ZERO

A New Approach to
NON-ALCOHOLIC DRINKS

THE ALINEA GROUP

Allen & Sarah
HEMBERGER

Nick
KOKONAS

Grant
ACHATZ

Micah
MELTON

TABLE OF CONTENTS

MISE EN PLACE

6	_	Zero Introductions
8	_	A Culinary Approach to Beverage Design
18	_	Before We Begin
22	_	Basic Syrups

BACK BAR — *page 25*

38	_	Amaro
29	_	American Whiskey
35	_	Aromatic Bitters
36	_	Bitter Amaro
42	_	Bitter Liqueur
41	_	Fernet
28	_	Gin
40	_	Herbal Liqueur
37	_	Jamaican Rum
32	_	Mezcal
34	_	Orange Bitters
31	_	Orange Liqueur
33	_	Spanish Rum
39	_	Sweet Vermouth
30	_	Tequila

CLASSIC COCKTAILS — *page 45*

54	_	Absinthe
60	_	Amaro & Coke
61	_	Bijou
59	_	Black Manhattan
50	_	Daiquiri
56	_	Death in the Afternoon
57	_	French 75
48	_	Grapefruit Mimosa
51	_	Jungle Bird
52	_	Margarita
62	_	Negroni
49	_	Paloma
58	_	Whiskey Sour

TABLE OF CONTENTS *continued*

MODERN COCKTAILS — *page 65*

130	Americano
92	BBQ
142	Bramblin' Man
94	Bubblegum
120	Celery Serrano
68	Cereal Killer
84	Down to Earth
100	Golden Glow
144	Green Papaya Salad
124	Instant Oatmeal
158	IPA
98	Juniper Raisin
82	Korean Spiced Margarita
152	Lovely Bunch
156	Me & You
164	Mole
110	Mum's The Word
102	New Millennium
86	Paprika Milk Punch
140	Pechuga
138	Pretzel
88	Return of the MAC
162	Rhubarb, Thyme, Juniper
106	Roasted Sweet Potato
74	Salad
150	Salted Caramel Cherry
146	Self-Carbonating Cinnamon Passionfruit Fizz
76	Shake Your Tamarind
116	Smoked Strawberry Old Fashioned
148	Snap Pea
78	Sparkling Plum Sour
108	Sparkling White Chocolate & Guava Consommé
134	Summer Summer
132	Sweet Corn
114	Thai Fighter
118	Thai Peanut Sauce
126	Watermelon Ginger Tonic
70	What Would Honeydew

WINES — *page 167*

176	_	Banana Chai
198	_	Blueberry Pancakes
180	_	Cardamom Port
170	_	Grapefruit Jicama Champagne
174	_	Grapefruit Turmeric Shrub
202	_	Green Herb Shrub
194	_	Lychee Champagne
196	_	Peach Shrub
182	_	Room For Dessert?
184	_	Rose Champagne
188	_	Spiced Blueberry Shrub
190	_	Strawberry Tomato
186	_	Sun Dried
172	_	Truffled Cherry
204	_	Umami Bomb

ETCETERA — *page 207*

214	_	$5 Shake
208	_	Breakfast Stout
212	_	Chicha Morada
220	_	Hong Kong Milk Tea
228	_	Leche De Tigre
222	_	Lemon Horchata
234	_	Limoncello
210	_	Olive Oil
226	_	Peanut Butter & Banana Sandwich
232	_	Soft Cider
218	_	Tzatziki

INDEX — *page 237*

ZERO
INTRODUCTIONS

"Hey everyone... welcome to Alinea."

My sisters and I smiled giddily as Chef Grant Achatz greeted us. We had been planning this dinner together for months and our big night had finally arrived. "Hi Chef," I managed, trying hard not to seem too starstruck.

"You guys hungry?" Chef asked, a slight smirk appearing on his face.

"Definitely!" my sister Rachel exclaimed.

"Awesome. I'm gonna go get to work. Devin here will be taking care of you tonight... I'll leave you in his hands."

Chef glided away as Devin seamlessly stepped in. "Hi there," he greeted us warmly. "We're going to start you off with a couple of bites from the kitchen. While we're waiting for those to arrive, may I ask if you'd like some wines to pair with your courses tonight?"

Rachel and I nodded eagerly, but my other sister, Emily, hesitated. "Uh, no...not for me tonight," she sighed as she unconsciously rubbed her stomach. "Can I just have... water, I guess?"

Devin's eyes twinkled. "No problem, I got you," he smiled reassuringly, stepping away from the table and disappearing through a nearby door. He returned moments later; balanced effortlessly on his fingers was a tray carrying three wine flutes and two bottles.

"We'll start you two off tonight with some Champagne," he said to Rachel and I, filling a pair of the flutes and offering them to us.

"And for you," he said, turning to Emily, "some 'champagne'." Devin paused to offer air quotes before filling the third flute with something that looked almost identical to the sparkling wine he'd offered Rachel and I. "We make this with rose hips, basil, and grapefruit peel. A little jicama juice gives it a nice tannic quality that works really well with the first course we'll be serving."

Emily beamed.

As Devin again stepped away, my sisters and I clinked our glasses before sipping from them. Rachel and I exchanged nods as we appraised our wines; they were predictably tasty. Then, after a brief pause, we turned to Emily.

"Hey can we taste that crazy stuff he brought you?"

It's not uncommon to have a guest visit one of The Alinea Group's restaurants who – for any number of reasons – may not wish to consume alcohol. Because Chef Achatz and Nick want these guests to enjoy the same high-level experience and careful consideration as anyone else who may dine with them, much care is given to the creation of thoughtfully-conceived non-alcoholic options. Rather than relying on obvious offerings like sodas, juices, or water, the chefs here seek to leverage their culinary experience to come up with something more complex and surprising.

Challenging themselves in this way has afforded the team interesting creative opportunities, and as they've explored, they've found themselves largely in uncharted waters. They've created... what, exactly? The chefs have concocted delicious drinks with complex, often-surprising layers of flavor. Some have been designed to pair with food and to serve the same purpose of elevating the dining experience as that of a fine wine. Others are light, refreshing, and great as stand-alones. They've made beverages that mimic the tones of wine or classic cocktails. But most are their own thing altogether... originals.

The more they've experimented, the more the team here has become intrigued. What should these creations be called? The chefs realized at one point that they'd outgrown their own lexicon – they couldn't find a good description that fully-encompassed the range of what they were making. When discussing them amongst themselves now, the term they tend to use is simply "non-alcoholics", or "NAs".

Fashioning a delicious, satisfying non-alcoholic drink is an opportunity to embrace constraint and to craft something unique and memorable. By removing one fundamental ingredient – alcohol – from their beverage pantry, Chef Achatz and his team have opened themselves up to new avenues for creativity. While the art of designing alcohol-free beverages may seem an arcane one, it's something that makes complete sense within the larger context of this restaurant group. In many ways, these creations are a natural extension of what the chefs here already do: they are simply flavors, combined thoughtfully, which happen to be expressed in liquid rather than solid form.

In sharing these recipes, we collectively wish to share our enthusiasm for curiosity, experimentation, and thoughtful hospitality. Whether the occasion be a dinner party, a holiday gathering, or an evening at home with a loved one, you and each of your guests – drinkers and abstainers alike – can enjoy something unique, well-crafted, and satisfyingly delicious. As with so many things in life, the effort involved is more than worth it.

— ALLEN
with The Alinea Group

A CULINARY APPROACH TO BEVERAGE DESIGN

To understand the process of designing a non-alcoholic drink, we find it helpful to first consider those which actually contain alcohol. Throughout the expansive world of beers, wines, and cocktails, alcohol itself is usually balanced with varying amounts of sweetness, bitterness, and/or acidity. Each of these elements is adjusted to bring the flavors of a given drink into harmony with one another.

Simply removing alcohol from this equation – certainly the easiest and most straightforward approach to creating non-alcoholic drinks – can dramatically throw off the balance of the drink. Consider, as an example, the traditional daiquiri cocktail; a mixture of rum, lime juice, and simple syrup. In the right proportions, each of these three ingredients stands in perfect balance with the others. If we simply remove the rum, the drink becomes both bitingly acidic and cloyingly sweet. We can replace the missing rum with water, but in so doing, we now have a drink that has lost much of its original complexity.

Why is this? The rum in a daiquiri contributes to the drink in several important ways. If it's a white rum, it may carry the mild, grassy flavors of the sugar cane from which it was made. If the rum was aged, it would also offer sweet caramel and molasses notes from the time it spent in a barrel. Jamaican rums often feature funky flavors of roasted banana or tropical fruits. These flavors are carried by the alcohol in the rum, which itself offers a tingling burn and a mouth-coating viscosity. While replacing this complex spirit outright with water may fill the glass to the same level, the water itself offers none of the rum's complex characteristics.

Discerning the qualities imparted by alcohol, then, helps us understand what roles would need to be filled in its absence.

It's also worth considering the context in which alcoholic beverages are consumed. Drinking alcohol is an optional, recreational activity – no one *needs* to drink alcohol simply to quench their thirst. Cocktails, wines, or beers are often consumed as part of an occasion: a party with friends, a meal with a loved one, or simply a relaxing moment after a day at work. The drink itself is often part of a fuller experience – taking note of this encourages us to ask how the absence of alcohol affects that experience.

One significant peculiarity of alcohol is that it tends to extend the time taken to consume a drink. Sweetened juices like our hypothetical rumless daiquiri often bring to mind the refreshing qualities of lemonade on a hot day, and thus end up being consumed quickly, without much regard for nuance or flavor. The same is true of many carbonated mixers, which are often reminiscent of soda pop. The relative flavor complexity of beer, wine, or cocktails – in contrast – generally encourages these beverages to be enjoyed at a more leisurely pace. One of the biggest challenges in designing non-alcoholic beverages, then, is slowing the drinker down. Crafting something to be sipped at the same pace (and perhaps in the same company) as an alcoholic beverage means that we have to consider how to add enough interest back into the drinking experience to warrant thoughtful consumption.

To develop this interest, there are many factors we consider. Let's explore each of these in depth.

OCCASION

What is the occasion for which we are designing? Is our drink meant to be consumed during the day or in the evening? Indoors or out? Hot weather or cooler temperatures? Will we serve more than one portion? Will it be paired with food or enjoyed on its own? Will there be other drinks before or after it? What will others be drinking, and how does this drink compare or contrast with that? How long would we like our drink to stay vital?

Questions like these can help determine how we will store and serve a drink, as well as what flavors, textures, and temperatures we might want to feature. Our bright and refreshing *Watermelon Ginger Tonic* recipe (page 126) is fantastic on a summery patio but might seem a bit odd if served alongside a dessert, whereas the funky earthiness of *Umami Bomb* (page 204) is best enjoyed as part of a meal. Considering the full context of the drinking experience can provide a toehold for further exploration.

FLAVOR & AROMA

Our creative process of balancing flavors and aromas is drawn from our culinary perspectives as chefs; it's a thing we do day in and day out as we prepare meals for guests each night. Our approach to combining flavors for drinks, then, is almost exactly the same as it is for food. Flavor is flavor, and we reason that if some flavors go well together in solid form, they are likely to harmonize in liquid form as well.

We have a fondness in our kitchens for utilizing unusual ingredients, and for combining familiar ingredients in unfamiliar ways. Building complexity in this way generally encourages our guests to explore the flavors with curiosity and surprise, which can in turn lead to a memorable dining experience. We often adopt the same strategy when designing non-alcoholic drinks.

One of the primary ways we accomplish this is by looking beyond the typical flavors offered by wines, beers, or cocktails and drawing inspiration from the culinary world as a whole. If the complex flavors that go into a Mexican mole sauce (page 164) or a crisp summer salad (page 74) are delicious in their usual form, can we manipulate them slightly to make them just as satisfying when served as a drink? Can we articulate the delicious, comforting aroma of instant oatmeal in liquid form (page 124)? While many of the flavor combinations in the recipes that follow may seem unusual, almost all of them can be traced back to a familiar culinary origin.

Once you've made the leap to thinking about drink flavors in this way, you're likely to find no shortage of inspiration from which to draw. What was one of your favorite childhood meals? Would rebuilding it as a drink benefit from the added ingredients of surprise and nostalgia? Are there regional cuisines or family recipes you can leverage in your creative process? Rather than serving fries and ketchup with your grilled burgers or blackberry cobbler for dessert, can you express these same flavors as a beverage? No question is too absurd to be worth exploring.

VISUAL AESTHETICS

Consider a small tumbler of orange juice. At a glance, its visual appearance is easy to understand; a guest has likely seen this before, and can anticipate a quick and refreshing drinking experience. But suppose we present the same juice in a wine glass. It's unusual that a person chugs a glass of wine with the same ease as a glass of oj. The simple matter of changing the visual presentation of the drink can provoke different associations and expectations.

Wines, beers, and cocktails each tend to have a distinctive "look" when served. Wines are presented in recognizable stemware, cocktails can feature eye-catching garnishes, and beers are often served in clear pint glasses that show off their color and the quality of their foams. In the context of alcoholic beverages, the visual presentation of a drink is often tied to other elements of it – bulbous wine glasses capture and focus the nuanced aromas of a complex wine, cocktail garnishes accent flavors, etc. The form of the presentation is usually tied to its function.

When crafting non-alcoholic drinks, an awareness of the visual language of alcoholic beverages helps us curate the drinking experience more thoughtfully. We can choose to honor (or violate) expectations of flavor, texture, temperature, and so on by the way we choose to assemble and present a drink. If we design a beverage inspired by a full-bodied Barolo – with assertive flavors of dried fruits, licorice, and chocolate – but then serve it in a small coupe glass with a cocktail pick laden with blackberries, we are setting different expectations than were we to present the same drink in a large red wine glass. No presentation is "right" or "wrong", we just want to make sure it's chosen thoughtfully.

A Culinary Approach to Beverage Design, continued

TEXTURE

What does a cocktail, a wine, or a beer *feel* like inside the mouth? A dry champagne might be effervescently biting on the tongue, while the carbonation in a heavy stout might feel almost creamy in comparison. A freshly-shaken daiquiri might have small ice shards floating in it, but these may seem large relative to the fine, sandy texture of a frozen margarita. Some white wines might feel thin and cleansing, while big, bold reds can be more viscous, with "grippy" tannins. Should our drink coat the mouth, lingering for several moments after each sip, or should it cut through the opulent richness of a dish with which we might pair it?

Acknowledging the wide range of mouthfeels that exist throughout the spectrum of alcoholic beverages lets us develop a curiosity about controlling it in any drink we design.

FORM FACTOR

The form in which we choose to present a non-alcoholic drink is highly dependent on the drinking experience we're interested in providing. A drink that has the look and feel of a cocktail may be perfectly delicious and satisfying, but could provide a slightly jarring drinking experience if served, say, at a dinner in which all other guests are enjoying wine pairings. We may choose, in such a case, to present the same flavors in the form of a wine instead. Contrastingly, a drink containing dark, roasted flavors (such as those in *Pretzel*, page 138) may be challenging and unusual if served in the form of a wine, but might be immediately recognizable if carbonated and served as a beer.

A Culinary Approach to Beverage Design, continued

SEASONING & BALANCE

In the context of cooking, we think of seasoning as the act of adjusting salt, sweetness, acidity, and bitterness to enhance – but not overwhelm – the underlying flavors of a given dish. A strawberry may taste like a better version of itself with a small addition of sugar; a tomato can seem more "tomato-y" with a sprinkle of salt. Seasoning allows us to bring all the elements of a dish into harmonious balance.

We approach the seasoning of drinks in the same way. Most everyone is familiar with the idea that the nearly-unpalatable juice of a fresh lemon can be rendered delicious with the addition of some water and sugar. This same principle applies to drinks, especially if we are building them up from scratch.

Seasoning becomes particularly important when considering the broader drinking experience of a beverage. If a drink is meant to be served with food, it likely needs to be balanced differently than if it were meant to be drunk on its own. A drink paired with a rich, fatty dish may benefit from the addition of a bit of extra acidity to help cut through the mouth-coating properties of the dish, refreshing the palate for the next bite. Similarly, a dessert beverage may need more or less sweetness to sit alongside its food pairing in a pleasant way. There are, unfortunately, no hard and fast rules for how to appropriately season a drink. Ultimately, your own palate needs to be your guide. If something tastes off to you, try adjusting sweetness, acidity, bitterness, salinity, or water levels – a bit at a time – until you find an ideal balance for your own sense of taste.

Most of the recipes in this book have been broken into components, with seasoning (acids, salt, sugar, and bitterness) added separately from the main flavor-building steps. With a few exceptions, we've balanced most drinks so that they taste nice when consumed on their own. If you plan to serve a drink with food (or you simply find the balance not quite to your liking), adjust the seasoning to taste.

A Culinary Approach to Beverage Design, continued

SERVING SIZE

The portion size of cocktails, wines, and beers is related to how flavorful these drinks are. If a beverage is aggressively flavorful, a large glass of it may grow to be overwhelming and unappetizing. When designing drinks, we consider how assertive (or subtle) our flavor profile is, and adjust our serving size accordingly.

TEMPERATURE

The serving temperature of a drink directly affects how its flavors need to be balanced.

Cocktails are frequently shaken or stirred with ice, which chills them to near-freezing temperatures. These temperatures tend to anesthetize the palate, muting flavors that might seem much more prominent when a drink is warmer. Chilling a cocktail with ice also necessarily imparts some amount of dilution – as ice chills, it melts. Because of these factors, we often need to exaggerate flavors and over-season a drink (which is to say: we'll use more acid, sugar, or bitterness) when serving it as a cocktail.

At warmer temperatures, flavors tend to become more pronounced, and consequently need to be balanced differently. White wines and beers are often chilled to refrigerator temperatures, which can be as much as 20°F (10°C) higher than those of cocktails. Red wines are frequently served at cellar or room temperature, and some cocktails (particularly winter-seasonal ones) are served warm.

ICE

While wines and beers are typically consumed "neat", cocktails are often served on ice. Ice plays a critical role not only in chilling the drink, but in rendering the high alcohol content of most cocktails palatable by way of dilution. As we discuss in more depth in *The Aviary Cocktail Book*, this dilution is not necessarily a bad thing – the potency of high-alcohol spirits can be overwhelming to the palate, and additional water creates space for other flavors to be built into a drink.

The aggressive character of alcohol is obviously not a factor in the context of non-alcoholic drinks, but it's still useful to devote some consideration to the role that ice may play in drink. Chilling quality aside, the use of ice presents us with an opportunity to *add* flavor, rather than taking it away. "Why make a soup with water," our chefs like to ask, "when you can make it with stock instead?"

Creating flavored ice is something we've experimented with extensively at The Aviary, and the concept is equally useful for non-alcoholic drinks. The general idea is pretty simple: create two well-balanced cocktails whose flavors pair well with one another, then freeze one of them. Stirring or shaking a drink with flavored ice allows us to push more flavor into a drink while simultaneously chilling it. Serving a drink on flavored ice offers us the added ability to modify the flavor profile of a cocktail as it's being consumed. We can inject surprising elements like heat, spice, vegetal, or herbal notes that flourish as the cocktail ages. Our *Margarita* (page 52), for example, grows more fruity and peppery over time through the use of Fresno chili-flavored ice cubes. A refreshing blend of cucumber and lime in *What Would Honeydew* (page 70) becomes more complex when we add pearls of ice made with melon and peppermint.

We can also control the rate of this flavor change. If we fully-chill a drink before pouring it over flavored ice, the ice will melt more slowly, leading to a very gradual flavor change. Abbreviating our shaking or stirring time, however, allows the cocktail to melt the ice in the glass as the drink further chills itself, releasing a sudden burst of flavor in the first few sips.

Beyond the choice of flavors, there are other questions about ice that are worth asking. Should the ice melt quickly or slowly? Will it be chewed or eaten as the drink is consumed, like many enjoy doing with soft pellet ice? Even if we're not using the ice as "flavor real estate", we want to recognize that its quality affects the overall drinking experience.

A Culinary Approach to Beverage Design, continued

CLARITY

Imagine sipping a glass of perfectly clear liquid that tastes exactly like warm hot chocolate – the experience would likely be surprising. Clarity is tied to the texture and viscosity of a beverage; transparent liquids usually offer a crisp, cleansing drinking experience, while opaque liquids are often thicker, with a mouth-coating quality that causes flavors to linger. Some cocktails have a cloudy appearance because of the inclusion of fresh citrus juices or small ice shards. The clarity (or lack thereof) of a liquid sets some expectations about flavor and mouthfeel before a guest ever takes a sip.

There are several ways one may clarify a cloudy liquid; we present several in the recipes that follow. These range from the simple act of letting a liquid sit in the refrigerator overnight for particles to settle to the bottom of a container, to more involved (but not necessarily difficult) techniques like gelatin clarification or using fining agents. While the clarity of a drink can affect the overall drinking experience, the step of clarifying a liquid (both in the following recipes and in your own experiments) is a matter of preference.

PROOF

Pure alcohol offers a "heat", a harshness, a welcome but sharp causticity. This heat is a peculiar one; it burns the lips and throat in a unique way, and fades noticeably between sips. The omission of alcohol in a non-alcoholic drink forgoes this distinctive experience.

It can be, therefore, worth exploring other ways to replicate this. In some of the recipes we share here, we employ various ingredients intended to simulate this heating sensation. Each have their own onset and falloff characteristics, and sometimes we mix and match to add extra complexity. We admit that we've found it challenging to precisely recreate the heat characteristics of alcohol, which only means there's a lot of opportunity for experimentation with this.

BEFORE WE BEGIN

While the majority of the recipes in this book originated within fine-dining restaurant environments, everything we share here has been re-written and rigorously tested to be made with reasonable ease at home. The following is meant to offer a bit of helpful information to help you get started.

BASIC EQUIPMENT

The recipes in this book describe the use of a combination of kitchen and bar tools. While most of these are commonly available, the following deserve special mention:

Blender

Many low-cost consumer blenders are bought solely for the purposes of crushing ice or making smoothies, and while they may work fine for these purposes, they can be problematic when used for different ingredients that are heat-sensitive or require higher power. Making rice milk for horchata, for example, requires a blender that can quickly break up rice grains without overheating the mixture (which causes it to thicken in an unpleasant way). Other considerations include the workable minimum and maximum volumes the blender can efficiently blend, and how effectively the shape of the blender pitcher directs ingredients towards the appliance's spinning blades.

There is considerable variation in the performance of consumer blenders, which makes it tricky to offer fail-safe prescriptions for blending some items in these recipes. We use durable, high-powered Vitamix blenders in our kitchens; depending on which model is in your own kitchen, you may find that you need to adjust blending times or speeds if something isn't behaving as you think it should. If lengthening blending times, be sure to stay mindful of the temperature of your ingredients; you rarely want to "cook" them (at least, for the recipes here).

Carbonation Device

The Perlini cocktail shaker is a specialized device that allows one to shake a drink with ice, carbonate it, and strain it all from one container. This sophisticated tool offers a high degree of control over the amount of carbonation that can be applied to a liquid. At home, an inexpensive hand-held soda carbonator, such as the Hamilton Beach Fizzini or the iSoda DrinkMake, also work well, with easy cleanup after use.

Cocktail Mixing Glass

Also sometimes referred to as a cocktail stirring glass or tin, these containers are used to stir portions of cocktails with ice to chill them. Easy substitutes for these include a pint glass, a measuring cup, or a small mixing bowl (basically anything that can contain ice and some liquid).

Cocktail Shaker Tin

The aeration and small ice shards that result from shaking a cocktail with ice add textural interest to the beverage. The tool we use for this in our bar is a Koriko brand weighted stainless steel shaking tin – it is both durable and easy to clean. At home, a mason jar with a lid is an easy substitute.

Digital Scale

Digital scales are inexpensive and precise; we use them to measure almost every ingredient in our kitchens. Not only do they offer a high degree of accuracy, they have the added benefit of dirtying fewer dishes. Rather than soiling multiple measuring cups and spoons, simply weigh all your ingredients into a single container, zeroing (or "taring") the scale between each ingredient addition. When shopping for one of these tools, look for a scale that supports measurements accurate to ½ gram.

Ice Molds

We have a slight obsession with collecting and using ice molds to create a wide variety of frozen shapes for our ice, and we invite you to be adventurous when exploring this yourself. A common mold used in this book is a 1¼ inch silicone cube mold, easily found online.

Jigger

The standard tool for measuring ingredients for individual portions of cocktails, we use stainless steel, Japanese-style conical jiggers with indicator markings included on the inside surface. Small measuring cups with markings accurate to ¼ oz can be used just as easily, or – in a pinch – measuring spoons (1 tbsp = ½ oz).

Juicer

Among the most commonly-used tools in this book is an electric juicer. This powerful device allows us to go beyond pre-made, bottled liquids and enables us to create our own. There are two main types of electric juicer:

Centrifugal juicers extract juice by shredding an ingredient with tiny spinning blades; they are particularly effective with fibrous or stringy products such as ginger or celery.

Masticating juicers forcefully press an ingredient against a mesh with a tapered rotating auger. These efficient juicers excel at extracting liquid from leafy greens and other delicate products without introducing excessive heat.

Either of these types of juicer will work equally well for the recipes in this book. Note that unless specified otherwise in our recipes, the resulting liquid needs to be strained through a fine mesh strainer after being extracted to ensure the final drink has a smooth, pleasing texture.

Many recipes call for the use of fresh citrus juices. These can be produced with the use of a hand-held citrus press, a citrus reamer, or (in a pinch) a good forceful squeeze. As is the case with an electric juicer, don't forget to strain the resulting juice through a mesh strainer to remove pulp or seeds.

Peelers/Graters

Y-Shaped Peelers – we use these inexpensive peelers to remove large citrus peels for garnish or expression.

Channel Knife – used to remove thin "laces" of peel from citrus fruits.

Microplane – available in a variety of sizes, these inexpensive and highly effective tools can be used for grating just about anything, from delicate fine citrus zest to hard spices.

Straining Tools

When we need to strain solids from a liquid, we do so using one of two tools:

A **mesh strainer**, which consists of a conical or domed metal mesh and which usually has a handle.

A **cocktail strainer**, often referred to as a "Hawthorne strainer", which has a spring mechanism that can be used to adjust how finely or coarsely to strain small ice shards when pouring shaken drinks from cocktail tins.

RECIPE STRUCTURE

Because we are building beverages from the ground up, our recipes tend to be structured more like those found in cookbooks rather than those found in typical cocktail guides. We typically break recipes into "components", each of which can be made ahead of time and stored until the drink is ready to be assembled and served. This is a practice drawn from how we work in our kitchens; it allows us to prepare everything we need before we open our doors for the day, so that we can serve drinks quickly and efficiently once guests arrive.

We find that expressing ingredients by weight is often the tidiest and most efficient way to work in both professional and home kitchens. You'll sometimes see, however, that we use volume measurements when portioning individual drinks. This is because the jigger is typically the most familiar measuring tool in the context of cocktails.

Before We Begin, continued

INGREDIENTS & SUBSTITUTIONS

Part of the experience we seek to provide guests who visit any of our restaurants is an element of surprise; one of the ways we accomplish this is through the use of ingredients that a guest may find unusual. We try to look beyond products that are commonly available at nationwide supermarket chains. Instead, we routinely explore offerings of local purveyors here in Chicago, as well as those we discover while traveling.

In the recipes that follow, we've sought to balance our fondness of unusual products with the feasibility of making these at home. Some of the ingredients called for will not be easily found in your local supermarket. These are, however, straightforwardly found online with the aid of your favorite search engine.

It can be tempting to consider substituting some of the more arcane items for those more easily (or quickly) found in your pantry or local grocery store. Substitutions are a fantastic first step towards making a recipe your own. We enthusiastically invite experimentation and deviation from what we present here, while offering the necessary caveat that the resulting beverage's flavor profile may be impacted accordingly. Be sure to taste and adjust your final creation and rebalance as necessary.

SERVING SIZE

While the notion of a "serving size" has a standardized meaning in a restaurant context, that phrase can have quite a bit of variance at home. Rather than specifying a "number of servings" for each recipe, we have scaled everything to yield roughly one quart (or one liter) in size, or "about enough to fill a large bottle" (which, incidentally, can be a very convenient storage container for your completed beverage batch). Halving or doubling a recipe to fit the needs of your occasion should work more or less as you'd expect it to.

SHELF LIFE & FOOD SAFETY

The use of fresh (rather than preserved, store-bought) ingredients in most of these recipes leaves them vulnerable to spontaneous fermentation, a process that inherently produces alcohol. This alcohol production is exacerbated by the additional use of sugar to balance the flavor of many of them. If you notice fizzing, bubbles, or a soda-pop-like hiss when opening a container of a non-alcoholic (and non-carbonated) beverage, chances are it has begun to ferment and contains some amount of alcohol.

Fermentation is not – in and of itself – strictly dangerous. Fermentation can and does produce delicious flavors and is a wonderful culinary technique to explore. But the production of alcohol through fermentation is of concern to any guest who may have health issues related to it. For this reason, avoid storing any of these beverages at room temperature for long periods of time. They can generally stay stable for up to a week in the refrigerator, though many will begin losing some of their most volatile flavors after a day or two. If you need to reserve a completed batch for longer than this, most of our recipes can be stored safely in the freezer for several months.

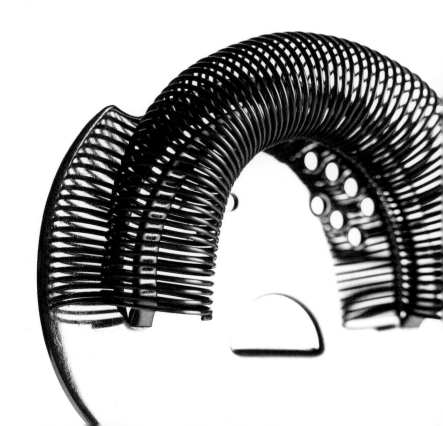

ASSEMBLING & SERVING COCKTAILS

While drinks that are meant to be presented as wines or beers can simply be poured and served, cocktails typically require a bit of assembly. Classic alcoholic cocktails are usually mixed to order and are often chilled to below-freezing temperatures (a feat made possible by the high alcohol content, which depresses the freezing point of the mixture) by being shaken or stirred with ice. This process is part of the cachet of cocktails, and assembling one at home is often part of the enjoyment.

When dealing with non-alcoholic cocktails, however, some differences need to be noted. For food safety reasons, we advise storing all cocktail components in this book in the refrigerator until serving. This stands in contrast to most alcoholic spirits, which are often stored at room temperature. Chilling pre-refrigerated non-alcoholic cocktail components requires less ice, which in turn imparts less dilution into the drink. If too much ice is used, or if the drink is chilled too aggressively, the mixture can reach near-freezing temperatures and can begin to slush. And because the cocktail cannot be chilled to as low of a temperature as alcoholic cocktails can, the time that the drink stays within an ideal drinking temperature range can be shorter.

To compensate for these differences, we recommend using less ice than you might normally use when shaking or stirring alcoholic cocktails, and abbreviating your shaking or stirring times to avoid chilling the drink to the point of slushing. And while not strictly necessary, we often find that chilling your glassware or serving a non-alcoholic cocktail with ice can be useful for prolonging the amount of time it stays properly cold.

MISCELLANY

Here are a few definitions and explanations of terms, techniques, and conventions that are used throughout this book.

Unless specified otherwise, **all herbs and citrus juices should be fresh**.

To **split and scrape** a vanilla bean, halve it lengthwise with a sharp knife, then use the back edge of the knife to scrape the tiny seeds from the pod. Unless otherwise noted, use both the seeds and the pod in the recipe.

To **double strain a cocktail** is to pour it from a cocktail shaker through both a Hawthorne strainer and a fine mesh strainer in a single step. Generally the shaker tin and Hawthorne strainer are held in one hand, while the fine mesh strainer is held above the cocktail glass in the other hand. Double-straining removes ice shards from the cocktail.

To **dry shake a cocktail** is to shake it vigorously in a cocktail shaker without ice. This technique is typically meant to aerate a drink before adding ice, which encourages a more frothy final result.

To **throw a cocktail**, gather two shaker tins or other durable containers that are large enough to comfortably hold a cocktail portion. Fill one container halfway with ice, and place a cocktail strainer into the container to hold the ice in place. Pour the cocktail portion into the other container. Gently pour the cocktail from one container into the other, back and forth several times. This technique allows you to aerate a cocktail while chilling it in a less violent way than shaking it will. Note that the more distance you can manage between the containers, the more aeration you can impart into the drink.

To **express a citrus peel**, grasp it between your thumb and forefinger, with the exterior of the peel facing away from your hand. Holding the peel close to the cocktail, pinch it firmly, which will cause a fine mist of oil to spray from the peel onto the beverage. The peel can then be either discarded or used as a garnish.

Many of these recipes can separate and settle over time. This is perfectly normal; you may choose to either pour off and store the clarified liquid or simply shake the drink to reincorporate the solids before serving, depending on your preferences for clarity and texture.

Before We Begin, continued

BASIC SYRUPS

Syrup is one of the most fundamental ingredients used to adjust the balance of a beverage. Raw sugar is difficult to dissolve in chilled liquids (a phenomenon you may have experienced if you've ever tried stirring a packet of sugar into a glass of iced tea or iced coffee). Syrups – composed of a sugar pre-dissolved into a liquid – allow the addition of sugar to a beverage easily, without the need to heat or agitate the drink.

In general, the syrups we use in the following recipes fall into one of two categories. "Simple" syrups are a mixture of sugar and liquid combined in a 1:1 ratio by weight. "Rich" syrups are similar, but combined in a ratio of 2 parts sugar to 1 part liquid. The extra sugar in rich syrups necessitates more heat and agitation to fully dissolve the sweetener. Rich syrups generally find the most use in cocktail-style beverages.

Many recipes for simple syrup instruct equal measures of sugar and water to be combined in a pot and brought to a boil on a burner. We find that this induces evaporation (as the water simmers and boils, it necessarily transforms into steam and leaves the pot), which can ultimately result in a syrup that is not actually equal parts water and sugar. While not critically important in a home kitchen, the potential differences that arise from different cooking times and temperatures are very important in restaurant kitchens, where we need to ensure day-to-day consistency. We avoid this problem by whisking sugar into warm tap water.

SIMPLE SYRUP

100g sugar
100g warm water

Combine the sugar and water in a medium bowl. Whisk to completely dissolve the sugar. Transfer to an airtight container and reserve in the refrigerator.

DEMERARA SYRUP

200g demerara sugar
100g water

In a small saucepan, stir together the sugar and water over medium heat just until the sugar is completely dissolved. Remove from the heat, cover, and let cool. Transfer to an airtight container and reserve in the refrigerator.

Chapter One

BACK BAR

CLASSIC COCKTAILS

MODERN COCKTAILS

WINES

ETCETERA

A NON-ALCOHOLIC BACKBAR

The backbar – the shelves behind a cocktail bar that are typically lined with bottles of spirits used to build drinks – is the pantry of the bartender. From base spirits like whiskey or gin to esoteric amari or housemade bitters, the backbar offers a wide array of flavors that can be combined in countless interesting ways. It seems fitting, then, that we begin our exploration of non-alcoholic beverage design by first assembling our own pantry from which we can work.

We begin our development of each of these recipes by first studying several examples of a given alcoholic spirit – say, rum or tequila – and trying to pick apart the drinking experience provided by each. What we try to tease out are elements like constituent flavors, the balance of sweetness and bitterness, viscosity, finish, etc. This study is admittedly challenging – we have to do the oral equivalent of squinting, tasting "through" the causticity of the alcohol itself, reaching beyond its heat to identify the other unique elements of the spirit. Tasting multiple examples of each type of spirit contemporaneously and diluting the samples in varying amounts can help with this process.

The recipes that follow are ones we've designed to work as substitutions in classic cocktail recipes. We wish to make it clear up front, however, that it's unlikely any of them would be mistaken for their alcoholic counterparts – such is not our intent. Rather, we seek to craft interesting and complex building blocks with which we can begin to assemble beverages.

Each of the following recipes yields approximately 1 qt (1 L).

In the style of
GIN

- 300 g vegetable glycerin
- 150 g juniper berries
- 150 g water
- 750 g water
- 17 g coriander seeds
- 17 g lemon peel, removed with a peeler
- 5 g fennel seeds
- 4 g cinnamon sticks, coarsely crushed
- 3 g fresh ginger, peeled and sliced thinly against the fibers
- 2 g star anise, coarsely crushed
- 1 g angelica root
- 1 g green cardamom seeds
- 1 g kosher salt

To make juniper tincture, combine the glycerin, juniper, and 150 g water in a blender, and pulse once or twice to break up some of the berries (take care not to purée the mixture). Transfer to an airtight container, and allow to steep in the refrigerator overnight. The following day, strain the mixture through a fine mesh strainer, discarding solids. Set this aside.

If you have sous vide equipment:
Combine 750 g water with all remaining ingredients in a vacuum bag and seal. Cook en sous vide at 90°C (195°F) for 1 hour. Meanwhile, prepare an ice bath. Transfer the bag to the ice bath to chill completely.

If you don't have sous vide equipment:
Combine 750 g water with all remaining ingredients in a medium saucepan, and bring the mixture to a boil over high heat. Cover the pot and reduce the heat to maintain a slow simmer for 1 hour. Remove from heat and let cool completely.

Strain the mixture through a fine mesh strainer, discarding solids. Add 250 g of the juniper tincture to the strained liquid, stirring to combine. Transfer to an airtight container and reserve in the refrigerator.

- 60 g malted barley
- 1 banana
- 1500 g water
- 75 g dried peaches
- 75 g dried figs
- 60 g unsalted popped popcorn
- 45 g charred american oak chips
- 37 g fenugreek seeds
- 34 g molasses
- 30 g cinnamon sticks, coarsely crushed
- 2 whole vanilla beans
- 1.5 g kosher salt

In the style of

AMERICAN WHISKEY

Preheat an oven to 400°F (205°C). Gather two small sheet trays or rimmed cookie sheets.

Spread the malted barley on one of the sheet trays, and place this into the oven. Toast the barley for 30 minutes, stirring occasionally to ensure even browning.

Meanwhile, line the other sheet tray with parchment or a silicone baking mat. Using a sharp knife, cut several small slits into the unpeeled banana and transfer it to the prepared sheet tray. Place this in the oven as well, and roast the banana for 15 minutes, or until the peel turns black.

When the items are done, remove each from the oven and allow them to cool completely. Chop the banana (with its skin still on) into small pieces.

If you have sous vide equipment:
Combine the barley and banana with all remaining ingredients in a vacuum bag and seal. Cook en sous vide at 90°C (195°F) for 1 hour. Meanwhile, prepare an ice bath. Transfer the bag to the ice bath to chill completely.

If you don't have sous vide equipment:
Combine the barley and banana with all remaining ingredients in a medium saucepan, and bring the mixture to a boil over high heat. Cover the pot and reduce the heat to maintain a slow simmer for 1 hour. Remove from heat and let cool completely.

Strain the mixture through a fine mesh strainer, discarding solids. Transfer the strained liquid to an airtight container and reserve in the refrigerator.

- ½ pineapple, skin on
- 1000 g water
- 40 g fresh apricot, pit removed, coarsely chopped
- 30 g agave syrup
- 20 g roasted unsalted peanuts
- 12 g whole black peppercorns, coarsely cracked
- 2 g kosher salt
- 2 whole vanilla beans, split and scraped
- 50 g fresh parsley leaves and stems
- 25 g fresh ginger, peeled and sliced thinly against the fibers
- 15 g fresh mint leaves and stems
- 9 g lime peel, removed with a peeler
- 7 g fresh jalapeño, seeds and stems removed, coarsely chopped
- 4 g fresh bay leaves

In the style of

TEQUILA

Using a sharp knife, remove the outer bark of the pineapple half (reserve the interior fruit for another use). Chop the pineapple bark coarsely into small pieces.

Combine the pineapple bark with the water, apricot, agave syrup, peanuts, peppercorns, salt, and vanilla.

If you have sous vide equipment:
Place the above ingredients in a vacuum bag and seal. Cook en sous vide at 90°C (195°F) for 1 hour. Meanwhile, prepare an ice bath. Transfer the bag to the ice bath to chill completely.

If you don't have sous vide equipment:
Place the above ingredients in a medium saucepan, and bring the mixture to a boil over high heat. Cover the pot and reduce the heat to maintain a slow simmer for 1 hour. Remove from heat and let cool completely.

Strain the mixture through a fine mesh strainer, discarding solids. Add the remaining ingredients and muddle to incorporate. Allow to steep at room temperature for 2 hours. Strain the mixture through a fine mesh strainer once again, discarding solids. Transfer the strained liquid to an airtight container and reserve in the refrigerator.

- 650 g fresh whole oranges (including peels), cut into quarters
- 550 g water
- 450 g sugar
- 2 whole cloves
- 4 g cinnamon sticks, coarsely crushed
- 1 whole vanilla bean, split and scraped

ORANGE LIQUEUR

(Inspired by Triple Sec, Cointreau)

If you have sous vide equipment:
Combine all ingredients in a vacuum bag and seal. Cook en sous vide at 90°C (195°F) for 4–6 hours, or until oranges are very soft. After this time, prepare an ice bath. Transfer the bag to the ice bath to chill completely.

If you don't have sous vide equipment:
Heat a large pot of water to about 90°C (195°F). Combine all ingredients and seal in a heavy-duty zip-top bag, trying to remove as much air as possible before closing. Dip the bag into the heated water, taking care to keep it off the bottom of the pot so the plastic doesn't burn (you can clip it to the side of the pot using a clothespin to help with this). Heat the bag for 4–6 hours, adjusting the burner as necessary to maintain a reasonably steady temperature. After this time, prepare an ice bath. Transfer the bag to the ice bath to chill completely.

Strain the mixture through a fine mesh strainer, discarding solids. Transfer the strained liquid to an airtight container and reserve in the refrigerator.

- ½ pineapple, skin on
- 1000 g water
- 40 g fresh apricot, pit removed, coarsely chopped
- 30 g agave syrup
- 25 g liquid smoke
- 10 g roasted unsalted peanuts
- 10 g coriander seeds
- 7 g whole black cardamom pods, coarsely crushed
- 8 g whole black peppercorns, coarsely cracked
- 4.5 g whole white peppercorns, coarsely cracked
- 2.5 g whole Szechuan peppercorns
- 2.5 g kosher salt
- 2 g Rare Tea Cellar Forbidden Forest Lapsang Souchong
- 20 g fresh parsley leaves and stems
- 20 g fresh ginger, peeled and sliced thinly against the fibers
- 5 g fresh jalapeño, seeds and stems removed, coarsely chopped
- 4 g fresh bay leaves
- 2 g lime peel, removed with a peeler

In the style of
MEZCAL

Using a BBQ grill or a gas burner, char the outer bark of the pineapple until it blackens. Allow it to cool completely, then remove the bark and chop it coarsely. Reserve the inner flesh for another use.

Combine the charred pineapple bark with the water, apricot, agave syrup, liquid smoke, peanuts, coriander, cardamom, peppercorns, salt, and lapsang souchong.

If you have sous vide equipment:
Place the above ingredients in a vacuum bag and seal. Cook en sous vide at 90°C (195°F) for 1 hour. Meanwhile, prepare an ice bath. Transfer the bag to the ice bath to chill completely.

If you don't have sous vide equipment:
Place the above ingredients in a medium saucepan, and bring the mixture to a boil over high heat. Cover the pot and reduce the heat to maintain a slow simmer for 1 hour. Remove from heat and let cool completely.

Strain the mixture through a fine mesh strainer, discarding solids. Add the remaining ingredients and muddle to incorporate. Allow to steep at room temperature for 2 hours. Strain the mixture through a fine mesh strainer again, discarding solids. Transfer the strained liquid to an airtight container and reserve in the refrigerator.

- 60g sugar
- 3 whole vanilla beans, split and scraped
- 25g orange peel, removed with a peeler
- 7g cacao nibs
- 3g nutmeg, coarsely cracked
- 2g salt
- 1000g water

In the style of

SPANISH RUM

In a medium saucepan, melt the sugar over medium-high heat until it is caramelized, taking care not to let it burn or begin to smoke. Add the vanilla, orange peel, cacao nibs, nutmeg, and salt, stirring for about 30 seconds, or until fragrant. Slowly add the water, stirring to combine. Bring the mixture to a boil, then cover and remove from heat. Allow to steep for 1 hour. Strain the mixture through a fine mesh strainer, discarding solids. Transfer the strained liquid to an airtight container and reserve in the refrigerator.

BLACKSTRAP RUM

To make blackstrap rum, stir in 80g molasses after removing the mixture from the heat.

- 500g water
- 50g vegetable glycerin
- 25g gentian root
- 20g coriander seeds
- 20g dried orange peel
- 8g star anise pods, coarsely crushed
- 5g whole cloves
- 5g whole green cardamom pods, crushed
- 4g cinchona bark
- 1.5g caraway seeds

ORANGE BITTERS

(Inspired by Regans' Orange Bitters)

If you have sous vide equipment:
Combine all ingredients in a vacuum bag and seal. Cook en sous vide at 90°C (195°F) for 1 hour. Meanwhile, prepare an ice bath. Transfer the bag to the ice bath to chill completely.

If you don't have sous vide equipment:
Combine all items in a medium saucepan, and bring the mixture to a boil over high heat. Cover the pot and reduce the heat to maintain a slow simmer for 1 hour. Remove from heat and let cool completely.

Strain the mixture through a fine mesh strainer, discarding solids. Transfer the strained liquid to an airtight container and reserve in the refrigerator.

- 40g sugar
- 60g whole cloves
- 40g cinnamon sticks, coarsely crushed
- 40g gentian root
- 11g star anise
- 7g dried orange peel
- 5g whole nutmeg, coarsely cracked
- 4.5g whole green cardamom pods, crushed
- 4g dried ginger powder
- 4g whole allspice, coarsely crushed
- 3g whole black peppercorns, coarsely cracked
- 1 whole vanilla bean, split and scraped
- 1g dried sassafras or sarsaparilla root, coarsely chopped
- 1000g water

AROMATIC BITTERS

(Inspired by Angostura Aromatic Bitters)

In a medium saucepan, melt the sugar over medium-high heat until it is slightly burned and just beginning to smoke. Add all remaining ingredients except water and toast for about 10 seconds, then carefully add the water (the mixture can splatter, so do this slowly). Cover the pot and bring the mixture to a boil, then lower the heat and maintain a slow simmer for 1 hour. Remove from the heat and allow the mixture to cool completely. Strain the mixture through a fine mesh strainer, discarding solids. Transfer the strained liquid to an airtight container and reserve in the refrigerator.

BACK BAR

- 1000g water
- 500g whole artichokes, roughly chopped
- 200g sugar
- 200g Coca-Cola
- 36g fresh basil leaves and stems
- 20g gentian root
- 18g cinchona bark
- 7g dried tarragon
- 6g angelica root

BITTER AMARO

(Inspired by Cynar)

Combine the water and artichokes in a blender, and blend on high speed for 30 seconds. Pour this mixture into a shallow pan and allow to sit uncovered for 2 hours, stirring frequently. The mixture will aggressively oxidize, turning nearly black. After this time, strain the mixture through a fine mesh strainer, discarding solids. Measure out 700g of the liquid and set it aside.

In a medium saucepan, melt the sugar over medium-high heat until it is deeply caramelized, but do not let it burn or begin to smoke. Slowly add very small amounts of the strained artichoke liquid at a time, swirling the pot between each addition to incorporate it into the sugar. Repeat this process until the liquid is no longer boiling, then add the remaining artichoke liquid and all remaining ingredients. Bring the mixture to a boil, cover, and lower the heat to maintain a slow simmer for 1 hour. Remove from heat and let cool completely.

Strain the mixture through a fine mesh strainer, discarding solids. Transfer the strained liquid to an airtight container and reserve in the refrigerator.

- 2 bananas
- ½ pineapple, skin on
- 1000 g water
- 21 g lime peel, removed with a peeler
- 13 g fresh ginger, peeled and sliced thinly against the fibers
- 10 g toasted oak wood chips
- 10 g whole black cardamom pods, crushed
- 5 g whole allspice, coarsely crushed
- 5 g cinnamon sticks, coarsely crushed
- 1 g kosher salt

In the style of

JAMAICAN RUM

Preheat an oven to 350°F (175°C). Line a sheet tray with parchment or a silicone baking mat. Using a sharp knife, cut several small slits into each unpeeled banana and transfer them to the prepared sheet tray. Roast the bananas in the oven for 20 minutes, or until the peels turn black. Remove from the oven and allow to cool completely. Chop the bananas (with the skin still on) into small pieces. Set these aside.

Using a sharp knife, remove the outer bark of the pineapple half (reserve the interior fruit for another use). Chop the pineapple bark coarsely into small pieces.

If you have sous vide equipment:
Combine all ingredients in a vacuum bag and seal. Cook en sous vide at 90°C (195°F) for 1 hour. Meanwhile, prepare an ice bath. Transfer the bag to the ice bath to chill completely.

If you don't have sous vide equipment:
Combine all items in a medium saucepan, and bring the mixture to a boil over high heat. Cover the pot and reduce the heat to maintain a slow simmer for 1 hour. Remove from heat and let cool completely.

Strain the mixture through a fine mesh strainer, discarding solids. Transfer the strained liquid to an airtight container and reserve in the refrigerator.

- 300g sugar
- 17g French chicory
- 12g cinnamon sticks, coarsely crushed
- 9g coriander seeds
- 8g angelica root
- 6g fennel seeds
- 5g gentian root
- 4g anise seeds
- 0.5g whole cloves
- 750g water
- 50g orange peel, removed with a peeler

AMARO

(Inspired by Averna Amaro)

In a medium saucepan, melt the sugar over medium-high heat until it is slightly burned and just beginning to smoke. Add all spices and roots and toast for about 10 seconds. Slowly add very small amounts of the water at a time, swirling the pot between each addition to incorporate it into the sugar. Repeat this process until the liquid is no longer boiling, then add the remaining water and the orange peel. Cover the pot and bring the mixture to a boil, then lower the heat and maintain a slow simmer for 1 hour. Remove from heat and allow mixture to cool completely. Strain the mixture through a fine mesh strainer, discarding solids. Transfer to an airtight container and reserve in the refrigerator.

- 100 g sugar
- 700 g water
- 200 g verjus rouge
- 2 whole vanilla pods, split and scraped
- 40 g fresh ginger, peeled and sliced thinly against the fibers
- 36 g dried figs, roughly chopped
- 25 g dried cherries
- 24 g orange peel, removed with a peeler
- 18 g lemon peel, removed with a peeler
- 16 g raisins
- 9 g cinnamon sticks, coarsely crushed
- 4 g coriander seeds
- 2 g whole green cardamom pods, crushed
- 2 g gentian root
- 1 g whole cloves
- 1 g dried chamomile
- 1 g cinchona bark
- 0.5 g dried tarragon

In the style of

SWEET VERMOUTH

In a medium saucepan, melt the sugar over medium-high heat until it is slightly burned and just beginning to smoke. Slowly add very small amounts of the water at a time, swirling the pot between each addition to incorporate it into the sugar. Repeat this process until the liquid is no longer boiling, then add the remaining water and all remaining ingredients. Cover the pot and bring the mixture to a boil, then lower the heat and maintain a slow simmer for 1 hour. Remove from heat and allow mixture to cool completely. Strain the mixture through a fine mesh strainer, discarding solids. Transfer to an airtight container and reserve in the refrigerator.

HERBAL LIQUEUR

(Inspired by Chartreuse)

- 750 g water
- 200 g honey
- 150 g vegetable glycerin
- 50 g fresh poblano peppers, stems and seeds removed, roughly chopped
- 50 g fresh ginger, peeled and sliced thinly against the fibers
- 50 g mastic
- 30 g fresh basil leaves and stems
- 25 g fresh parsley leaves and stems
- 20 g galangal, peeled and sliced thinly against the fibers
- 18 g coriander seeds
- 12 g star anise, coarsely crushed
- 10 g fennel pollen
- 8 g dried fennel seeds
- 7 g dried tarragon
- 7 g whole green cardamom pods, crushed
- 7 g fresh thyme leaves and stems
- 7 g orange peel, removed with a peeler
- 5 g lemon peel, removed with a peeler
- 5 g whole black peppercorns, coarsely cracked
- 5 g cinnamon sticks, coarsely crushed
- 4 g fenugreek seeds
- 3 g dried mint
- 3 g whole Szechuan peppercorns
- 2.5 g whole green peppercorns, coarsely cracked
- 1 g whole cloves
- 0.1 g saffron threads

If you have sous vide equipment:
Combine all ingredients in a vacuum bag and seal. Cook en sous vide at 90°C (195°F) for 1 hour. Meanwhile, prepare an ice bath. Transfer the bag to the ice bath to chill completely.

If you don't have sous vide equipment:
Combine all items in a medium saucepan, and bring the mixture to a boil over high heat. Cover the pot and reduce the heat to maintain a slow simmer for 1 hour. Remove from heat and let cool completely.

Strain the mixture through a fine mesh strainer, discarding solids. Transfer the strained liquid to an airtight container and reserve in the refrigerator.

- 100 g sugar
- 1000 g water
- 85 g galangal, peeled and sliced thinly against the fibers
- 30 g cane syrup
- 30 g fresh mint leaves and stems
- 20 g dried mint
- 8 g aloe vera leaf powder
- 6 g gentian root
- 6 g cinchona bark
- 4 g whole green cardamom pods, crushed
- 0.1 g saffron threads

In the style of

FERNET

In a medium saucepan, melt the sugar over medium-high heat, and continue cooking until it is fully burned and smoking. Slowly add very small amounts of the water at a time, swirling the pot between each addition to incorporate it into the sugar. Repeat this process until the liquid is no longer boiling, then add the remaining water and all remaining ingredients. Cover the pot and bring the mixture to a boil, then lower the heat and maintain a slow simmer for 1 hour. Remove from the heat and allow the mixture to cool completely. Strain the mixture through a fine mesh strainer, discarding solids. Transfer to an airtight container and reserve in the refrigerator.

- 700g water
- 400g sugar
- 180g fresh grapefruit (including peel), roughly chopped
- 100g fresh orange (including peel), roughly chopped
- 12g gentian root
- 10g cinnamon sticks, coarsely crushed
- 6g whole pink peppercorns, coarsely cracked
- 5g star anise, coarsely crushed
- 4g angelica root
- 1.5g whole cloves
- 1g red food coloring (optional)

BITTER LIQUEUR

(Inspired by Campari)

If you have sous vide equipment:
Combine all ingredients in a vacuum bag and seal. Cook en sous vide at 90°C (195°F) for 1 hour. Meanwhile, prepare an ice bath. Transfer the bag to the ice bath to chill completely.

If you don't have sous vide equipment:
Combine all items in a medium saucepan, and bring the mixture to a boil over high heat. Cover the pot and reduce the heat to maintain a slow simmer for 1 hour. Remove from the heat and let cool completely.

Strain the mixture through a fine mesh strainer, discarding solids. Transfer the strained liquid to an airtight container and reserve in the refrigerator.

Chapter Two

BACK BAR

CLASSIC COCKTAILS

MODERN COCKTAILS

WINES

ETCETERA

In this section, we make use of the building blocks of our backbar pantry (see previous section) by substituting them into classic cocktail recipes.

Creating non-alcoholic riffs of classic cocktails tends to be easier in some cases than in others. We've found, for example, that bright, refreshing drinks like the *Grapefruit Mimosa* (page 48) or the *Margarita* (page 52) tend to resemble their alcoholic counterparts reasonably closely, whereas very spirit-forward, high-proof drinks like the *Negroni* (page 62) or the *Black Manhattan* (page 59) offer much more of a challenge to replicate seamlessly. As a rule of thumb, we find that the more central of a role a high-proof spirit plays in the flavor of a classic cocktail, the more work we need to do to replace its absence with a comparable level of interest and complexity.

The following recipes are just a small sample of ways to combine our backbar ingredients, and just as with the backbar recipes themselves, there is a lot of room for further experimentation.

CLASSIC COCKTAILS

CLASSIC COCKTAILS

GRAPEFRUIT MIMOSA

1oz (30ml) fresh grapefruit juice, chilled
4oz (120ml) lychee champagne – *page 194*

Pour the grapefruit juice into a tall champagne flute. Top with lychee champagne. Serve.

CLASSIC COCKTAILS

PALOMA

3 oz (90 ml) tequila – *page 30*
1 oz (30 ml) fresh grapefruit juice
¾ oz (22.5 ml) simple syrup – *page 22*
¾ oz (22.5 ml) fresh lime juice
1 grapefruit peel,
  removed with a peeler

Fill a tall serving glass halfway with ice. Combine all ingredients except grapefruit peel with ice in a cocktail shaker. Shake vigorously, then strain into the serving glass. Express the grapefruit peel over the glass, then garnish the glass with the peel. Serve with a straw.

CLASSIC COCKTAILS

DAIQUIRI

3oz (90ml) Spanish or Jamaican rum – *pages 33 & 37*
¾oz (22.5ml) fresh lime juice
¾oz (22.5ml) simple syrup – *page 22*
1 grapefruit peel

Combine all ingredients except the peel with ice in a cocktail shaker. Shake vigorously, then strain into a medium serving glass. Express the grapefruit peel over the glass, then discard the peel. Serve.

JUNGLE BIRD

2½oz (75ml) Spanish or Blackstrap rum – *page 33*
1½oz (45ml) fresh pineapple juice
¾oz (22.5ml) bitter liqueur – *page 42*
½oz (15ml) simple syrup – *page 22*
½oz (15ml) fresh lime juice
1 maraschino cherry
1 orange peel, removed with a peeler

Fill a medium serving glass halfway with ice. Combine the rum, pineapple juice, bitter liqueur, simple syrup, and lime juice with ice in a cocktail shaker. Shake vigorously, then strain into the serving glass. Garnish with a maraschino cherry and an orange peel. Serve.

MARGARITA

3oz (90ml) mezcal – *page 32*
1oz (30ml) orange liqueur – *page 31*
¾oz (22.5ml) fresh lime juice

CLASSIC

Wipe the outside rim of a serving glass with a lime wedge. Holding the glass with the rim facing slightly downwards, sprinkle the outer rim of the glass with kosher salt.

Combine all ingredients with ice in a cocktail shaker. Shake vigorously, then strain into the serving glass. Serve.

WITH HOT SAUCE ICE

5 Fresno chilies, stems removed
510 g water
60 g fresh lime juice
30 g sugar

To make hot sauce ice, extract juice from the Fresno chilies with a juicer. Combine the juice with water, lime juice, and sugar, whisking to dissolve sugar. Fill 1¼ inch (3.2 cm) square ice mold with mixture. Freeze until completely solid.

To serve, place two hot sauce ice cubes in a medium serving glass. Combine mezcal, orange liqueur, and lime juice with ice in a cocktail shaker. Shake vigorously, then strain into the serving glass. Serve.

ABSINTHE

Absinthe – a sweet, strongly-alcoholic liqueur flavored primarily of anise and fennel – is fascinatingly complex. Used as an ingredient in cocktails, small amounts can contribute a delicious dash of *Je ne sais quoi* to a beverage. We built our recipe here in the form of a syrup, which allows us to store it easily and deploy it in small amounts during service.

For true absinthe enthusiasts, we also offer a method for doing an absinthe drip – a very traditional way of drinking absinthe in which cold water is slowly added to dilute the liqueur (or, in our case, syrup) to a more palatable concentration. As with traditional absinthe, this version will *louche* (turn cloudy) during this dilution process as the essential oils precipitate out of solution.

ABSINTHE SYRUP

- 250 g vegetable glycerin
- 24 drops sweet fennel oil
- 13 drops lemon oil
- 6 drops star anise oil
- 1 drop green food coloring

Combine all ingredients in a blender. Blend on high speed for 1 minute to dissolve oils. Transfer the mixture to an airtight container and reserve in the refrigerator.

Note: the syrup will be aerated and cloudy after blending; the tiny bubbles causing this will rise and dissipate over several days, clarifying the mixture. This is purely cosmetic; the syrup's flavor is not affected.

TO ASSEMBLE AND SERVE

- 10 g absinthe syrup
- 80 g water, very cold

Pour the syrup into a small serving glass. Slowly add cold water, stirring with a small spoon to dissolve the syrup. As the mixture combines, dissolved oils will come out of solution, creating a frosted, hazy appearance (this phenomenon is traditionally referred to as "the *louche*").

CLASSIC COCKTAILS

DEATH IN THE AFTERNOON

½ oz (15 ml) absinthe syrup – *page 55*
6 oz (180 ml) lychee champagne – *page 194*

Pour the absinthe syrup into a tall champagne flute. Add the lychee champagne, stirring gently to combine. Serve.

CLASSIC COCKTAILS

FRENCH 75

3 oz (90 ml) gin – *page 28*
¾ oz (22.5 ml) fresh lemon juice
¾ oz (22.5 ml) simple syrup – *page 22*
3 oz (90 ml) lychee champagne – *page 194*
1 lemon peel, removed with a peeler

Combine the gin, lemon juice, and simple syrup with ice in a cocktail shaker. Shake vigorously, then strain into a tall champagne flute. Top with lychee champagne. Express the lemon peel over the glass, then garnish glass with the peel. Serve.

WHISKEY SOUR

3 oz (90 ml) American whiskey – *page 29*
¾ oz (22.5 ml) fresh lemon juice
¾ oz (22.5 ml) simple syrup – *page 22*
1 egg white
1 lemon peel, removed with a peeler

Combine the whiskey, lemon juice, simple syrup, and egg white in a cocktail shaker. Dry shake vigorously to aerate. Add ice, shake again until chilled, then strain into a medium serving glass. Express the lemon peel over the glass, then discard the peel. Serve.

CLASSIC COCKTAILS

BLACK MANHATTAN

2oz (60ml) American whiskey – *page 29*
1oz (30ml) amaro – *page 38*
2 dashes aromatic bitters – *page 35*

Combine all ingredients with ice in a cocktail mixing glass. Stir until chilled and diluted, then strain into a medium serving glass. Garnish with two maraschino cherries. Serve.

CLASSIC COCKTAILS

AMARO & COKE

2 oz (60 ml) Coca-Cola, chilled
1 oz (30 ml) bitter amaro or fernet – *pages 36 & 41*

Fill a medium glass halfway with ice. Add Coca-Cola, then gently pour in amaro. Serve.

CLASSIC COCKTAILS

BIJOU

1oz (30ml) gin – *page 28*
1oz (30ml) herbal liqueur – *page 40*
1oz (30ml) sweet vermouth – *page 39*

Combine all ingredients with ice in a cocktail mixing glass. Stir until chilled and diluted, then strain into a medium serving glass. Serve.

CLASSIC COCKTAILS

NEGRONI

1oz (30ml) gin – *page 28*
1oz (30ml) sweet vermouth – *page 39*
1oz (30ml) bitter liqueur – *page 42*
1 orange peel, removed with a peeler

Combine the gin, vermouth, and bitter liqueur with ice in a cocktail mixing glass. Stir until chilled and diluted, then strain into a medium serving glass. Express the orange peel over the glass, then garnish glass with the peel. Serve.

BACK BAR

CLASSIC
COCKTAILS

Chapter
Three

MODERN
COCKTAILS

WINES

ETCETERA

MODERN COCKTAILS

While crafting non-alcoholic drinks that offer the familiarity of classic cocktails is an interesting challenge for us, we don't wish to constrain ourselves to just those flavors common to the bar world. If we allow ourselves to draw inspiration from the culinary world as well, our palette is considerably broadened.

The following section contains examples of drinks we've served in each of our restaurants. Some of these were designed as standalone beverages to be served at our modern cocktail bar, The Aviary, or in The Office, our classic speakeasy. Others have been crafted with the intent of being served alongside food at our restaurants: Alinea, Next, Roister, and St. Clair Supper Club. While our sources of inspiration are widely varied, our goal for each of these drinks is the same: we want to offer our guests something thoughtful, interesting, and delicious.

When following any of these recipes, taste as you work. Take note of the various elements of the drinking experience we discuss on pages 8–17. We encourage you to adjust any of these elements you might want to, pushing and pulling them around to make them your own.

CEREAL KILLER

MODERN COCKTAILS

This drink is loosely inspired by the venerable Manhattan – a classic cocktail made with whiskey, vermouth, and bitters. Despite having only three ingredients, a Manhattan offers incredible depth; trying to build something that offers a similar drinking experience is a fun challenge for us. Our riff relies on assertive, aromatic ingredients like toasted barley, blackberry, baking spices, and chocolate.

A note about the bitters used in this drink and elsewhere throughout this book: while Fee Brothers products are made using a vegetable-based glycerin (rather than the high-proof alcohol typically found in other bitters), they still contain trace amounts of alcohol, comparable to those found in the vanilla extracts used in baking. Our *Aromatic Bitters* (page 35) may be substituted to render the drink completely non-alcoholic.

BLACKBERRY SYRUP

200g fresh blackberries
150g sugar
100g water

Combine all ingredients in a small saucepan and bring to a boil over medium heat. Remove from heat, cover, and allow to cool completely. Strain the mixture through a fine mesh strainer, pressing on the berries to extract as much juice as possible. Discard solids. Transfer the liquid to an airtight container and reserve.

SPICED BARLEY STOCK

50g malted barley
33g cinnamon sticks, coarsely crushed
3g whole allspice berries
650g water

In a medium saucepan, toast the barley over high heat until fragrant. Add the cinnamon and allspice, and continue toasting until fragrant. Add the water, cover, and bring the mixture to a boil. Remove from heat and allow the mixture to steep for 1 hour. Strain the mixture through a fine mesh strainer, discarding solids. Transfer to an airtight container and reserve in the refrigerator to chill thoroughly.

CEREAL KILLER BATCH

475g spiced barley stock
110g blackberry syrup
70g POM pomegranate juice
70g Seedlip Spice 94
30g carob syrup
17g demerara syrup *(page 22)*
10g Fee Brothers Black Walnut Bitters
1.5g citric acid
0.5g kosher salt

Combine all ingredients in a medium bowl, whisking to dissolve acid and salt. Transfer to an airtight container and reserve in the refrigerator to chill thoroughly.

TO PORTION AND SERVE

Place a large chunk of ice into a medium serving glass. Add 4oz (120ml) of the chilled cocktail batch, stirring briefly to chill. Serve.

WHAT WOULD HONEYDEW

SMOKED SALT SOLUTION

100 g water
9 g smoked sea salt

In a small saucepan, bring the water and smoked salt to a simmer over medium heat, stirring to dissolve salt. Remove from heat and let cool completely. Strain through a fine mesh strainer, discarding any solids. Reserve.

CLARIFIED LIME CUCUMBER

2 English cucumbers
1½ limes
0.5 g angelica root
5 drops Pectinex Ultra SP-L
5 drops kieselsol
5 drops chitosan

Cut the cucumbers into 1 inch (2.5 cm) cubes, and extract the juice from these with a juicer.

Cut the limes (including peels) into small pieces. Combine the lime pieces, cucumber juice, angelica root, Pectinex, and kieselsol in a blender. Pulse three or four times to break up limes, taking care not to purée mixture. Transfer to a tall container and allow to steep at room temperature for 1 hour. Strain the mixture through a fine mesh strainer, discarding solids. Stir in the chitosan. Cover and allow the mixture to settle in the refrigerator for 3–4 hours, or until solids settle to the bottom of the container. Gently pour off the clarified liquid, leaving as much sediment as possible behind. Reserve in an airtight container in the refrigerator.

What Would Honeydew, continued

What Would Honeydew, continued

MINT HONEYDEW ICE

- 490 g fresh honeydew juice, extracted with a juicer
- 55 g glucose
- 45 g water
- 45 g verjus blanc
- 0.5 g salt
- 12 drops non-alcoholic peppermint extract

Combine all ingredients in a medium bowl, whisking to dissolve the glucose and salt. Fill a ½ inch (1.3 cm) spherical ice mold with the mixture. Freeze until completely solid. Reserve.

WHAT WOULD HONEYDEW BATCH

- 335 g aloe vera juice
- 205 g clarified lime cucumber
- 135 g verjus blanc
- 95 g sugar
- 1.5 g smoked salt solution
- 0.5 g orange flower water

Combine all ingredients in a mixing bowl, whisking to dissolve sugar and salt. Transfer to an airtight container and reserve in refrigerator to chill thoroughly.

TO ASSEMBLE AND SERVE

- 4 oz (120 ml) chilled what would honeydew batch

Fill a medium serving glass halfway with mint honeydew ice marbles. Combine the chilled cocktail batch with ice in a cocktail shaker. Shake briefly, then double-strain into the serving glass over the ice. Serve.

SALAD

MARINATED TOMATOES

- 8 grape tomatoes
- 5g extra virgin olive oil
- 3.5g sherry vinegar
- 1g garlic, finely minced
- 0.1g black pepper, coarsely ground

Prepare an ice bath. Fill a large pot with water, and it bring to a boil. Cut a small × in the stem end of each tomato. Blanch the tomatoes in the boiling water for 5 seconds, then immediately transfer them to the ice bath. Using a paring knife, peel the tomatoes, discarding the skins.

In a small bowl, combine the remaining ingredients, stirring to mix. Add the peeled tomatoes and stir gently to coat. Allow the tomatoes to marinate for at least 1 hour. Reserve in a covered container at room temperature.

WALNUT PAPRIKA SYRUP

- 40g walnuts
- 240g sugar
- 200g water
- 1g smoked sweet paprika

In a medium saucepan, toast the walnuts over medium heat until fragrant. Add the remaining ingredients, cover, and bring to a boil. Remove from heat and let cool completely. Strain the mixture through a fine mesh strainer, discarding solids. Transfer the liquid to an airtight container and reserve in the refrigerator overnight to allow any remaining sediment to settle to the bottom of the container. The next day, gently pour the syrup into a clean container, leaving any settled solids behind. Reserve in the refrigerator.

SALAD BATCH

- 400g fresh green tomato juice, extracted with a juicer
- 150g verjus blanc
- 100g walnut paprika syrup
- 100g water
- 26g green olive brine (sometimes called "green olive juice")

Combine all ingredients in a mixing bowl. Transfer to an airtight container and reserve in the refrigerator to chill thoroughly.

TO ASSEMBLE AND SERVE

Pour 3oz (90ml) of the chilled cocktail batch into a medium serving glass. Garnish with one marinated tomato, a small basil leaf, and a flake of sea salt. Serve.

SHAKE YOUR TAMARIND

We developed this drink to pair with two spice-forward courses we served as part of our "Spice Trade" menu at Next in early 2019 (one was a pork belly dish with chili-spiked mole sauce; the other a salad featuring Vietnamese flavors). We wanted something full bodied, with an assertive ripeness to stand up to the powerful spiciness of the food.

TAMARIND CORIANDER STOCK

- 4g coriander seeds, coarsely crushed
- 0.5g cinnamon sticks, coarsely crushed
- 400g water
- 40g tamarind

In a medium saucepan, toast the coriander and cinnamon over medium heat until fragrant. Add the remaining ingredients and bring to a boil, stirring to break up and incorporate tamarind. Remove from heat, cover, and allow to steep for 20 minutes. Strain the mixture through a fine mesh strainer, discarding solids. Transfer to an airtight container and reserve in the refrigerator to chill thoroughly.

SHAKE YOUR TAMARIND BATCH

- 315g tamarind coriander stock
- 150g fresh pineapple juice, extracted with a juicer
- 120g water
- 115g Seedlip Garden 108
- 30g sugar
- 25g Maguey Sweet Sap
- 20g kalamansi purée
- 2g citric acid
- 1g kosher salt

Combine all ingredients in a mixing bowl, whisking to dissolve sugar, acid, and salt. Strain the mixture through a fine mesh strainer, discarding any solids. Transfer to an airtight container and reserve in the refrigerator to chill thoroughly.

TO PORTION AND SERVE

Pour 3oz (90ml) of the chilled cocktail batch into a medium serving glass. Serve.

SPARKLING PLUM SOUR

FRUITCAKE ICE

14g cinnamon sticks, coarsely crushed

3 green cardamom pods, coarsely crushed

3 whole cloves, coarsely crushed

1 small star anise pod, coarsely crushed

1 black cardamom pod, coarsely crushed

420g water

225g verjus rouge

102g prune juice

66g prunes, roughly chopped

45g dark brown sugar

42g dates, roughly chopped, pits included

40g dried figs, roughly chopped

2.5g fenugreek seeds

1.5g orange oil

1g sumac

1g orange zest, removed with a microplane

0.5g kosher salt

0.5g ajowan seeds

½ vanilla bean

In a medium saucepan, toast the cinnamon, black and green cardamom, cloves, and star anise over medium heat until fragrant. Add all remaining ingredients and bring to a boil, stirring to dissolve sugar and to combine everything thoroughly. Lower heat, cover, and simmer for 1 hour. Remove from heat and allow to cool completely. Strain the mixture through a fine mesh strainer, discarding solids. Fill a 1¼ inch (3.2 cm) square ice mold with mixture. Freeze until completely solid. Reserve.

Sparkling Plum Sour, continued

FALERNUM

- 3 g cinnamon sticks, coarsely crushed
- 2 g star anise
- 2 g allspice berries
- 1 g cloves
- 530 g water
- 170 g sugar
- 60 g raw cashews
- 7.5 g ginger, peeled and sliced thinly against the fibers
- ½ vanilla bean, split and scraped
- 1 g lime zest, removed with a microplane

In a medium saucepan, toast the cinnamon, star anise, allspice, and cloves over medium heat until fragrant. Add water, sugar, cashews, ginger, and vanilla. Bring to a boil, then remove pot from heat, cover, and allow to steep for 20 minutes. Add lime zest and allow to steep for an additional 10 minutes. Strain the mixture through a fine mesh strainer, discarding solids. Transfer to an airtight container and reserve in the refrigerator.

PLUM VERJUS

- 1 plum
- 190 g verjus blanc
- 50 g sugar

Halve plum and remove pit. Slice plum thinly.

If you have sous vide equipment:
Combine the plum slices, verjus, and sugar in a vacuum bag and seal. Cook en sous vide at 75°C (165°F) for 2 hours. Meanwhile, prepare an ice bath. Transfer the bag to the ice bath to chill completely. Strain the mixture through a fine mesh strainer, discarding solids. Transfer the strained liquid to an airtight container and reserve.

If you don't have sous vide equipment:
Bring a large pot of water to a simmer. Combine the plum slices, verjus, and sugar and seal in a heavy-duty zip-top bag, trying to remove as much air as possible before closing. Dip the bag into the simmering water, taking care to keep it off the bottom of the pot so the plastic doesn't burn (you can clip it to the side of the pot using a clothespin to help with this). Simmer the bag for about 2 hours. Meanwhile, prepare an ice bath. Transfer the bag to the ice bath to chill completely. Strain the mixture through a fine mesh strainer, discarding solids. Transfer the strained liquid to an airtight container and reserve.

Sparkling Plum Sour, continued

TO ASSEMBLE AND SERVE

1oz (30ml) plum verjus
¾oz (22.5ml) falernum
½oz (15ml) fresh lemon juice
1oz (30ml) water
2 dashes aromatic bitters *(page 35)*

Place 2 fruitcake ice cubes into a medium glass.

If you have a Perlini cocktail shaker:
Combine all ingredients with ice in a Perlini shaker. Shake vigorously until chilled and diluted. Invert the shaker and charge with CO_2 until the shaker is fully-pressurized and no more gas flows in. Shake the canister to dissolve gas. Allow the contents to settle for 30 seconds, then gently vent excess gas from the canister. Pour the carbonated cocktail over the fruitcake ice. Serve.

If you have a carbonation device:
Combine all ingredients with ice in a cocktail shaker. Shake vigorously until chilled and diluted. Double-strain into a carbonation device. Carbonate according to manufacturer's instructions, then gently pour the carbonated cocktail over the fruitcake ice. Serve.

If you do not have carbonation equipment:
Combine all ingredients with ice in a cocktail shaker. Shake vigorously until chilled and diluted. Double-strain into the serving glass over the fruitcake ice. Serve.

KOREAN SPICED MARGARITA

GINGER SYRUP

- 1 large hand ginger
- 100g sugar

Peel the ginger and slice thinly against the fibers. Extract juice from ginger using a juicer. Strain the juice through a fine mesh strainer, discarding solids. Let the juice sit for 1 hour to allow the starch to settle. Pour off the juice into a clean container, leaving as much starch behind as possible. Discard the starch.

Combine 100g of the ginger juice with the sugar in a blender. Blend on high speed until the sugar is completely dissolved. Transfer to an airtight container and reserve in the refrigerator.

GOCHUJANG SYRUP

- 110g mandarin purée
- 67g sugar
- 20g yuzu marmalade, strained of any solids
- 8.5g gochujang
- 1g citric acid

Combine all ingredients in a small bowl, whisking to dissolve sugar and acid completely. Reserve in an airtight container in the refrigerator.

BARLEY STOCK

- 120g barley
- 600g water

Preheat an oven to 400°F (205°C). Spread the barley on a sheet tray or cookie sheet and toast in the oven for 30 minutes, stirring occasionally to ensure even browning. Remove from the oven and let cool completely.

In a medium saucepan, combine the toasted barley and water, and bring to a boil over high heat. Remove from the heat, cover, and allow to steep for 1 hour. Strain the mixture through a fine mesh strainer, discarding solids. Reserve the liquid in an airtight container in the refrigerator.

CHILI POWDER MIX

- 10g coarse Korean chili powder
- 6g kosher salt
- 6g sugar
- 3g citric acid

Combine all ingredients in a small bowl, stirring to mix thoroughly. Transfer to a small airtight container and reserve.

KOREAN SPICED MARGARITA BASE BATCH

- 400g barley stock
- 200g gochujang syrup
- 135g Maguey Sweet Sap
- 70g demerara syrup (page 22)
- 60g ginger syrup
- 37g rice wine vinegar
- 3.5g red yuzu kosho

Combine all ingredients in a mixing bowl, whisking to mix thoroughly. Strain the mixture through a fine mesh strainer, discarding any solids. Transfer the liquid to an airtight container. Reserve in the refrigerator to chill thoroughly.

TO ASSEMBLE AND SERVE

- 4oz (120ml) chilled spiced margarita base
- ½oz (15ml) fresh lime juice

Wipe half of the outside rim of a serving glass with a lime. Holding the glass with the rim facing slightly downwards, sprinkle the chili powder mix onto the outer rim of the glass. Place two medium cubes of ice into the glass. Set the glass aside.

Combine the chilled cocktail base and lime juice with ice in a cocktail shaker. Throw the cocktail (see page 21) 4–5 times to chill and aerate it, then pour it into the prepared serving glass. Serve.

DOWN TO EARTH

Here we balance the earthy, vegetal flavors of mushrooms and celery with the crisp sweetness of jicama, which yields a drink that's both savory and sweet at once. Any mushrooms can be used in this drink; portabello or button mushrooms produce good yields when juiced, while more exotic varieties – like hen-of-the-woods or shiitake mushrooms – can add interesting flavor nuance. This cocktail works well with meaty dishes that include bacon, rabbit, or roast pork.

DOWN TO EARTH BATCH

300g fresh mushroom juice, extracted with a juicer
275g fresh jicama juice, extracted with a juicer
150g fresh celery root juice, extracted with a juicer
75g sugar
2g ascorbic acid
1.5g kosher salt

Combine the mushroom juice, jicama juice, and celery root juice in a medium saucepan. Cover and bring to a simmer. Remove from heat and add the remaining ingredients, whisking to dissolve the sugar, acid, and salt. Cover and allow the mixture to cool completely, then transfer it to an airtight container. Reserve in the refrigerator to chill thoroughly.

TO PORTION AND SERVE

1 orange peel, removed with a peeler

Pour 3oz (90ml) of the chilled cocktail batch into a small serving glass. Express the orange peel over the cocktail, then insert it into the glass. Serve.

PAPRIKA MILK PUNCH

SPICE MIX

- 4g cumin seeds
- 15g sugar
- 10g kosher salt

In a medium saucepan, toast the cumin seeds over medium heat until fragrant. Transfer the toasted seeds to a spice grinder and grind to a fine powder.

In a small bowl, combine the sugar, salt, and 2g of the toasted cumin powder, stirring to combine. Transfer to a small airtight container and reserve.

CLARIFIED MILK PUNCH

- 330g fresh orange juice
- 270g fresh red bell pepper juice, extracted with a juicer
- 17g smoked sweet paprika
- 3g citric acid
- 330g whole milk

Combine the orange juice, red pepper juice, paprika, and citric acid in a medium bowl, whisking to dissolve acid. Set aside.

In a small saucepan over medium heat, warm the milk gently just until it begins to steam, taking care not to allow it to boil. Remove from heat and pour into the paprika mixture – the milk should instantly curdle. Allow the mixture to cool, then cover and store in refrigerator at least overnight, or ideally for 48 hours for a more clarified final result.

Gather two large bowls. Set a fine mesh strainer over one bowl and begin pouring the curdled milk mixture into it. Milk curds will settle into the strainer and begin to form a filtration bed. As the mixture begins to run clear, move the strainer over the second bowl and continue straining. When finished, gently pour the reserved cloudy portion from the first bowl over the curds in the strainer into second bowl to further clarify it, taking care to disturb the curds as little as possible. Reserve the clarified liquid in the refrigerator.

PAPRIKA MILK PUNCH BATCH

- 515g clarified milk punch
- 260g water
- 26g sugar
- 3g citric acid
- 1.5g salt

Combine all ingredients in a mixing bowl, whisking to dissolve sugar, acid, and salt. Transfer to an airtight container and reserve in refrigerator to chill thoroughly.

TO ASSEMBLE AND SERVE

- 3oz (90ml) chilled paprika milk punch batch

Pour a small amount of olive oil into a shallow saucer. Spread the spice mix onto a second shallow saucer. Holding a medium serving glass upside-down, dip the rim first into the olive oil to moisten, then into the spice mix to coat the rim. Pour chilled cocktail batch into the glass. Serve.

RETURN OF THE MAC

One of our favorite ingredients to work with in the context of beverages is time. The window of time that exists between sips of a drink is an opportunity for us to change its flavors.

We play with this notion in many ways. The Porthole, for example, is a large, beautiful infusion vessel in which we serve cocktails designed to evolve and transform. We deliberately present this drink with small glasses, which throttle the rate at which the beverage is consumed and encourage periodic refills as the cocktail changes.

Return of the Mac, continued

MCINTOSH APPLE SLICES

- 200 g water
- 1 lemon wedge
- 1 McIntosh apple

In a medium bowl, squeeze the lemon wedge into the water and stir to combine. Halve the apple lengthwise and remove the core and seeds. Slice the apple thinly using a sharp knife or mandoline into half-moons about ⅛ inch (3 mm) thick. Immerse the slices in the acidulated water to prevent them from browning as you work. Remove the slices from the water and pat dry with a paper towel. Stack the slices and reserve them between damp paper towels in an airtight container in the refrigerator.

RETURN OF THE MAC BASE BATCH

- 280 g Seedlip Spice 94
- 220 g Martinelli's apple cider
- 120 g verjus blanc
- 80 g simple syrup *(page 22)*
- 40 g Mott's apple juice
- 12 g Maguey Sweet Sap
- 8 g POM pomegranate juice
- 1 g malic acid

Combine all ingredients in a medium bowl, stirring to mix thoroughly. Transfer to an airtight container and reserve in the refrigerator to chill thoroughly.

IN THE PORTHOLE

- 8 g Rare Tea Cellar Cider Spiced Noir tea
- 3.5 g dried hibiscus flowers
- 1 g whole allspice berries
- 25 whole black peppercorns
- 5 McIntosh apples slices
- 5 thyme sprigs
- 4 freeze-dried cranberries
- 4 green cardamom pods, gently crushed
- 1 whole orange peel, removed with a peeler, all pith removed
- 1 cinnamon stick

With the Porthole laying flat on its side, arrange all ingredients as you'd like, working from the largest ingredient to the smallest. Close the Porthole and ensure it is sealed tightly on both faces.

TO ASSEMBLE AND SERVE

Place the assembled Porthole on a tabletop, and fill with the reserved cocktail base to a level just below the bottom edge of the filter screen. Serve with small tasting glasses. At the table, invite guests to refill the tasting glasses from the Porthole periodically as it infuses.

BBQ

The universe of BBQ is vast and fiercely territorial. Depending on where one lives, "BBQ sauce" could describe anything from bright, mustardy flavors to the sharp tang of vinegar and spice. But perhaps the most widely recognized is that of a classic Kansas City-style sauce – a magical blend of smoke, tomato, brown sugar, vinegar, and a hodgepodge of spices and herbs.

We can express this complex flavor profile in cocktail form by creating a "stock" from a few classic spices found in many BBQ rubs. Instead of the ketchup that's traditionally found in most sauces of this style, we make use of strawberry juice, which adds some light sweetness (this "swap" of strawberries for tomatoes is a technique we also explore on page 190). The result is something complex and tasty, and which pairs excellently with, well, you can probably guess.

BBQ STOCK

- 5g cumin seeds
- 5g yellow mustard seeds
- 200g water
- 6g dried chipotles, seeds and stems removed

In a medium saucepan, toast the cumin and mustard seeds over medium heat until fragrant. Add the water and chipotles and bring to a boil. Remove from heat and allow to steep for 20 minutes. Strain the mixture through a fine mesh strainer, discarding solids. Transfer to an airtight container and reserve in the refrigerator to chill thoroughly.

CHARRED STRAWBERRIES

- 6–8 fresh strawberries, tops attached
- 10g sugar *(estimated)*

Slice strawberries in half lengthwise. Sprinkle the face of each half lightly with sugar. Using a small brûlée torch, char the face of each strawberry half until blackened. Let cool completely. Reserve.

BBQ BATCH

- 600g water
- 100g BBQ stock
- 70g fresh strawberry juice, extracted with a juicer
- 40g glucose
- 25g sugar
- 16g coconut aminos
- 3g citric acid
- 3 drops liquid smoke

Combine all ingredients in a mixing bowl, whisking to dissolve sugar and acid. Transfer to an airtight container and reserve in the refrigerator to chill thoroughly.

TO ASSEMBLE AND SERVE

Pour 3oz (90ml) of the chilled cocktail batch into a medium serving glass. Garnish the glass with one charred strawberry. Serve.

BUBBLEGUM

The ingredients that produce the flavor of classic bubblegum are closely-guarded manufacturer's secrets; they're often described as a mishmash of artificial flavors like strawberry, orange, banana, and other tropical fruits. While one can combine real fruits to produce something with a tasty, tropical fruit punch flavor, it's actually the "artificial-ness" of the flavors used in bubblegum that are key to its distinctive taste.

So how do we replicate this flavor? Why not make a stock using bubblegum?

We bolster the flavors of our bubblegum stock with passionfruit green tea and a syrup made from citrus peels, then balance the mixture with a bit of acidity to prevent the drink from being too cloying. The addition of glucose and glycerin add some viscosity to the drink; this texture helps support the flavors.

CITRUS OLEO SACCHARUM

1 lemon
1 navel orange
60g sugar
60g water

Peel the lemon and orange with a vegetable peeler, taking care to remove as little pith as possible. Reserve the fruit for another use.

In a medium bowl, combine 30g lemon peel, 30g orange peel, and sugar. Muddle the mixture with a spoon or a cocktail muddler. Cover and allow to sit for at least 4 hours or overnight, muddling and stirring periodically.

In a small saucepan, bring the water to a simmer. Pour the water over the citrus peels, stirring to dissolve sugar. Strain the mixture through a fine mesh strainer. Transfer to an airtight container and reserve in refrigerator.

PASSIONFRUIT TEA

500g water
20g Rare Tea Cellar Passion Fruit Dream Green Tea

Combine the water and tea in a medium bowl, stirring to mix thoroughly. Cover and allow to steep in the refrigerator overnight. The following day, strain the mixture through a fine mesh strainer, discarding solids. Transfer the tea to an airtight container and reserve in the refrigerator.

Bubblegum, continued

BUBBLEGUM STOCK

| 250 g water
| 62.5 g pink bubblegum

If you have sous vide equipment:
Combine the water and bubblegum in a vacuum bag and seal. Cook en sous vide at 80°C (175°F) for at least 4 hours.

If you don't have sous vide equipment:
Bring a large pot of water to a simmer. Seal the water and bubblegum in a heavy-duty zip-top bag, trying to remove as much air as possible before closing. Dip the bag into the simmering water, taking care to keep it off the bottom of the pot so the plastic doesn't burn (you can clip it to the side of the pot using a clothespin to help with this). Simmer the bag for about 4 hours.

Meanwhile, prepare an ice bath. Transfer the bag to the ice bath to chill completely. Using scissors, make a small incision in one corner of the bag. Drain contents through a fine mesh strainer, discarding any solids. Transfer the liquid to an airtight container and reserve in refrigerator.

Bubblegum, continued

BUBBLEGUM BATCH

- 352g passionfruit tea
- 244g bubblegum stock
- 48g glucose
- 42g citrus oleo saccharum
- 37.5g verjus blanc
- 15.5g vegetable glycerin
- 6g lactic acid

Combine all ingredients in a mixing bowl, whisking to mix thoroughly. Transfer the mixture to an airtight container. Reserve in refrigerator to chill thoroughly.

TO PORTION AND SERVE

Pour 3oz (90ml) of the chilled cocktail batch into a medium serving glass. Serve.

JUNIPER RAISIN

Delicious and refreshing on its own, the flavors in this effervescent drink also complement gamey meat dishes like venison, lamb, or duck.

JUNIPER RAISIN BATCH

- 214 g raisins
- 36 g juniper berries
- 800 g water
- 10 g sugar
- 3 g citric acid
- 2 g sumac
- 1 g kosher salt

Combine raisins and juniper berries in a food processor. Pulse a few times to break mixture into small pieces. Transfer to a medium heatproof bowl. In a medium saucepan, bring water to a boil. Pour 500 g boiling water over raisin juniper mixture, cover, and allow to steep for 10 minutes. Strain mixture through a fine mesh strainer into a clean bowl. Return raisins and juniper to original bowl. Bring remaining water to a boil again, and pour 250 g boiling water over raisin juniper mixture. Cover and allow to steep for 15 minutes. Strain mixture through a fine mesh strainer, combining both batches of strained liquids. Discard solids.

To the raisin juniper stock, add remaining ingredients, whisking to dissolve sugar, acid, and salt. Strain mixture through a fine mesh strainer, then through a tea strainer or 100-micron Superbag to remove fine particles. Transfer to carbonation device, and chill thoroughly in refrigerator or an ice bath. Carbonate according to manufacturer's instructions. Reserve in refrigerator.

TO PORTION AND SERVE

Fill a tall serving glass halfway with ice. Gently add 3 oz (90 ml) of the chilled cocktail batch. Serve.

GOLDEN GLOW

This drink offers an example of how clarity affects the drinking experience. Serving it immediately after preparing it yields a slightly thicker texture reminiscent of bottled tomato juice, which tends to make the drink "feel" more savory. Allowing the batch to settle overnight in the refrigerator yields a beautifully clarified liquid with a less viscous mouthfeel, which helps the drink feel bright and refreshing.

BLACK PEPPER STOCK

- 10 g whole black peppercorns, coarsely cracked
- 150 g water

In a medium saucepan, toast the peppercorns over medium heat until fragrant. Add the water and bring to a boil. Remove from heat, cover, and allow to steep for 20 minutes. Strain the mixture through a fine mesh strainer, discarding solids. Transfer to an airtight container and reserve in the refrigerator.

GOLDEN GLOW BATCH

- 455 g coconut water
- 125 g fresh yellow bell pepper juice, extracted with a juicer
- 65 g fresh yellow tomato juice, extracted with a juicer
- 65 g aloe vera juice
- 60 g passionfruit purée
- 35 g black pepper stock
- 20 g sugar
- 10 g red miso
- 0.5 g citric acid
- 0.5 g malic acid

Combine all ingredients in a mixing bowl, whisking to dissolve sugar and acids. Transfer to an airtight container and reserve in the refrigerator to chill thoroughly.

TO PORTION AND SERVE

Pour 3 oz (90 ml) of the chilled cocktail batch into a medium serving glass. Serve.

NEW MILLENNIUM

The *20th Century Limited* was an express passenger train that ran between Chicago and New York from 1902 through 1967, and served as the namesake for a popular cocktail during this era consisting of gin, vermouth, and crème de cacao. We served a modernized riff on this century-old classic for a period at our bar, The Aviary. Our version included a sweet vermouth infused with nectarines, and was served with a smoked watermelon popsicle (interested readers can find the recipe for this drink on page 244 of *The Aviary Cocktail Book*).

This simplified non-alcoholic version of that drink gains complexity by the use of rose and white grape juice. Intrepid chefs may add even more complexity by finding creative ways to add the white chocolate notes of crème de cacao used in the original 20th Century, and can replicate our watermelon ice pop by swapping the water in the Smoke Ice component for fresh watermelon juice. The carbonation step – as is the case in most of our carbonated recipes – is optional, but we find the added texture appealing.

LAPSANG SOUCHONG TEA

- 150 g water
- 4 g Rare Tea Cellar Forbidden Forest Lapsang Souchong

In a medium saucepan, bring water to a boil. Remove from heat. Measure 100 g of water into a separate bowl, and add tea. Cover and let steep for 5 minutes. Strain the tea through a fine mesh strainer, discarding solids. Transfer the liquid to an airtight container and reserve.

SMOKE ICE

- 530 g water
- 65 g lapsang souchong tea
- 30 g sugar
- 1.5 g red food coloring *(optional)*
- 1 g citric acid
- 0.5 g malic acid
- 0.5 g kosher salt

Combine all ingredients in a blender, and blend on high speed for 30 seconds. Strain through a fine mesh strainer. Fill 1¼ inch (3.2 cm) square ice mold with mixture. Freeze until completely solid. Reserve.

New Millennium, continued

NECTARINE WHITE GRAPE STOCK

- 364g nectarines
- 364g white grape juice

Halve nectarines and remove pits. Slice nectarines thinly.

If you have sous vide equipment:
Combine nectarines and white grape juice in a vacuum bag and seal. Cook en sous vide at 75°C (165°F) for 4 hours. Meanwhile, prepare an ice bath. Transfer the bag to the ice bath to chill completely. Strain the mixture through a fine mesh strainer, discarding solids. Transfer the strained liquid to an airtight container and reserve.

If you don't have sous vide equipment:
Heat a large pot of water to about 75°C (165°F) – or just hot enough that it's uncomfortable to dip your finger into it. Combine nectarines and white grape juice and seal in a heavy-duty zip-top bag, trying to remove as much air as possible before closing. Dip the bag into the heated water, taking care to keep it off the bottom of the pot so the plastic doesn't burn (you can clip it to the side of the pot using a clothespin to help with this). Heat the bag for about 4 hours, adjusting the burner as necessary to maintain a reasonably steady temperature. Meanwhile, prepare an ice bath. Transfer the bag to the ice bath to chill completely. Strain the mixture through a fine mesh strainer, discarding solids. Transfer the strained liquid to an airtight container and reserve.

NEW MILLENNIUM BASE BATCH

- 370g verjus blanc
- 90g sugar
- 4g rose hips
- 330g nectarine white grape stock
- 0.5g rose water

In a small saucepan, combine verjus, sugar, and rose hips, cover, and bring to a boil over medium heat. Remove from heat and let steep for 20 minutes. Strain mixture through a fine mesh strainer, discarding solids. Combine liquid with nectarine white grape stock and rose water, stirring to mix thoroughly. Transfer to an airtight container. Reserve.

New Millennium, continued

TO ASSEMBLE AND SERVE

4 oz (120 ml) new millennium base
1 oz (30 ml) fresh lemon juice
½ oz (15 ml) water
¼ oz (7.5 ml) simple syrup *(page 22)*

Place 2 smoke ice cubes into medium glass.

If you have a Perlini cocktail shaker:
Combine all ingredients with ice in a Perlini shaker. Shake vigorously until chilled and diluted. Invert the shaker and charge with CO_2 until the shaker is fully-pressurized and no more gas flows in. Shake the canister to dissolve gas. Allow the contents to settle for 30 seconds, then gently vent excess gas from the canister. Pour the carbonated cocktail into the serving glass over the ice. Serve.

If you have a carbonation device:
Combine all ingredients with ice in a cocktail shaker. Shake vigorously until chilled and diluted. Double-strain into a carbonation device and carbonate according to manufacturer's instructions. Gently pour the drink into the serving glass over the ice. Serve.

If you do not have carbonation equipment:
Combine all ingredients with ice in a cocktail shaker. Shake vigorously until chilled and diluted. Double-strain into the serving glass over the ice. Serve.

ROASTED SWEET POTATO

POMEGRANATE GREEN TEA

- 300 g water
- 20 g Rare Tea Cellar Pomegranate Green Dream tea

In a medium saucepan, bring the water to a boil. Remove from heat. Measure 250 g of the hot water into a separate bowl and add tea. Cover and let steep for 15 minutes. Strain the tea through a fine mesh strainer, discarding solids. Transfer the liquid to an airtight container and reserve.

FIG STOCK

- 100 g dried figs, coarsely chopped
- 450 g water

Place the fig pieces in a medium heatproof bowl. In a medium saucepan, bring the water to a boil. Remove from heat and pour 425 g of the hot water over the figs. Cover the bowl and allow to steep until completely cool. Strain the mixture through a fine mesh strainer, discarding solids. Transfer the liquid to an airtight container and reserve.

ROASTED SWEET POTATO PURÉE

- 1 sweet potato
- 100 g sweetened condensed milk

Preheat oven to 350°F (175°C). Line a sheet tray with a silicone baking mat. Using a sharp knife, cut several small slits into the peel of the potato, then wrap tightly in aluminum foil. Transfer to the prepared sheet tray. Roast the potato for 40 minutes, or until very tender when pierced with a fork. Let cool completely. Remove and discard peel.

Measure 200 g of the roasted sweet potato into a blender. Add the condensed milk, and blend on high speed for 30 seconds, or until smooth. Strain the mixture through a fine mesh strainer to ensure the purée is completely smooth. Reserve.

ROASTED SWEET POTATO BATCH

- 360 g fig stock
- 160 g roasted sweet potato purée
- 120 g pomegranate green tea
- 30 g dark brown sugar
- 25 g pomegranate molasses
- 1 g citric acid
- 0.5 g salt

Combine all ingredients in a mixing bowl, whisking to dissolve the sugar, acid, and salt. Transfer to an airtight container and reserve in the refrigerator until ready to serve.

TO ASSEMBLE AND SERVE

- 1 orange peel, removed with a peeler

Warm the cocktail batch gently in a microwave or on the stovetop. Pour 3 oz (90 ml) of the warm cocktail batch into a medium serving glass. Express the orange peel over the drink. Discard the peel. Serve.

SPARKLING WHITE CHOCOLATE & GUAVA CONSOMMÉ

A *consommé* is a type of soup – usually a stock made with animal bones or vegetables – that has been clarified using egg whites. As the egg whites cook in the simmering broth, they form a webby structure at the surface of the liquid that chefs refer to as a *raft*. This raft traps fat and other impurities in the liquid; once it has formed, it can be carefully removed, leaving behind a lovely transparent liquid.

While typically used in savory applications, there's no reason we can't use this technique to clarify sweet liquids. In this recipe, our raft helps us remove fat and small solids from white chocolate and guava. The egg whites also help add body to the liquid, which – when carbonated – forms a fragrant "head" of foam not unlike that of beer.

TREATED GUAVA PURÉE

350 g guava purée
11 g Pectinex Ultra SP-L

In a medium bowl, stir together the guava purée and Pectinex. Cover and allow the mixture to sit at room temperature for at least 4 hours before using.

WHITE CHOCOLATE GUAVA CONSOMMÉ

2 vanilla beans
300 g water
96 g white chocolate, coarsely chopped
300 g ice
300 g treated guava purée
50 g egg whites

Slice the vanilla beans in half lengthwise. Use the rear edge of the knife to scrape the seeds from each pod half.

Combine the water and white chocolate in a medium saucepan. Warm the mixture over medium heat to melt the chocolate, stirring constantly to prevent scorching. Remove from heat. Add the vanilla seeds, ice, and treated guava purée, stirring to combine. Allow the mixture to cool completely.

In a medium bowl, whisk the egg whites until very frothy. Combine the whites with the cooled white chocolate mixture, stirring to mix thoroughly. Transfer the mixture to a clean saucepan. Slowly bring the mixture to a simmer over medium heat; the egg whites will form a "raft", clarifying the mixture. Take care not to stir as this raft forms, to prevent it from breaking up. When the raft has fully formed and the mixture has clarified, gently remove it from heat.

Line a fine mesh strainer with several layers of cheesecloth. Strain the clarified consommé through the cheesecloth, discarding solids. Transfer the consommé to an airtight container. Reserve in the refrigerator.

SPARKLING WHITE CHOCOLATE & GUAVA CONSOMMÉ BATCH

530 g white chocolate guava consommé
230 g water
26 g sugar
3 g lactic acid
1.5 g citric acid

Combine all ingredients in a medium bowl, whisking to dissolve sugar and acids. Transfer to a carbonation device. Chill thoroughly in a refrigerator or an ice bath. Carbonate according to the manufacturer's instructions. Reserve in the refrigerator.

TO PORTION AND SERVE

Gently pour 4 oz (120 ml) of the chilled cocktail batch into a medium serving glass. Serve.

MUM'S THE WORD

Watermelon is one of our favorite ingredients to play with when the weather turns warm here in Chicago – its flavor is light, sweet, and deliciously refreshing. Here we complement this bright flavor with some additional notes of licorice, ginger, and chrysanthemum, which offer subtle and intriguing depth.

CHRYSANTHEMUM TEA

- 200 g water
- 15 g Rare Tea Cellar Emperor's Yellow Chrysanthemum

In a medium saucepan, bring the water to a simmer. Remove from heat. Measure 175 g of the hot water into a separate bowl and add the tea. Cover and let steep for 8 minutes. Strain the tea through a fine mesh strainer, discarding solids. Transfer the liquid to an airtight container and reserve.

STAR ANISE STOCK

- 10 g star anise, coarsely crushed
- 300 g water

In a medium saucepan, toast the star anise over medium heat until fragrant. Add water, cover, and bring to a boil. Remove from heat and allow to steep for 5 minutes. Strain the mixture through a fine mesh strainer, discarding solids. Transfer the liquid to an airtight container and reserve.

FIG STOCK

- 50 g dried figs, coarsely chopped
- 150 g water

Place the fig pieces in a medium heatproof bowl. In a medium saucepan, bring the water to a boil. Remove from heat, and pour 100 g of the hot water over the figs. Cover the bowl and allow to steep until completely cool. Strain the mixture through a fine mesh strainer, discarding solids. Transfer the liquid to an airtight container and reserve.

Mum's the Word, continued

MUM'S THE WORD BATCH

- 1 large thumb ginger
- 571g fresh watermelon juice, extracted with a juicer
- 54g chrysanthemum tea
- 51g fig stock
- 37g star anise stock
- 25g sugar
- 1g lime zest, removed with a microplane
- 1g malic acid
- 0.3g salt

Peel the ginger and slice thinly against the fibers. Extract juice from ginger using a juicer. Strain the juice through a fine mesh strainer, discarding solids. Let the juice sit for 1 hour to allow the starch to settle. Pour off the juice into a clean container, leaving as much starch behind as possible. Discard the starch.

Combine 5g of the ginger juice with the remaining ingredients in a mixing bowl, whisking to dissolve sugar, acid, and salt. Transfer to the refrigerator and allow the zest to infuse for at least 2 hours. Strain through a fine mesh strainer, discarding solids. Transfer the liquid to an airtight container. Reserve in the refrigerator to chill thoroughly.

TO PORTION AND SERVE

Pour 3oz (90ml) of the chilled cocktail batch into a medium serving glass. Serve.

THAI FIGHTER

THAI STOCK

- 15 g white sesame seeds
- 10 g coriander seeds
- 450 g water
- 80 g lemongrass
- 50 g ginger, peeled and sliced thinly against the fibers
- 5 dried kaffir lime leaves
- 1 Thai chili, seeds and stem removed, sliced thinly

In a medium saucepan, toast the sesame and coriander over medium heat until fragrant. Add the remaining ingredients and bring to a boil. Remove from heat and allow to steep for 12 minutes. Strain through a fine mesh strainer, discarding solids. Transfer to an airtight container and reserve in the refrigerator to chill thoroughly.

THAI FIGHTER BATCH

- 350 g Thai stock
- 125 g fresh pineapple juice
- 75 g fresh grapefruit juice
- 65 g sugar
- 50 g fresh lime juice

Combine all ingredients in a mixing bowl, whisking to dissolve sugar. Transfer to an airtight container and reserve in refrigerator to chill thoroughly.

TO ASSEMBLE AND SERVE

- 1 grapefruit twist, removed with a channel knife

Combine 3 oz (90 ml) of the chilled cocktail batch with ice in a cocktail shaker. Shake until chilled and diluted, then double-strain into a medium glass. Garnish with a grapefruit twist. Serve.

SMOKED STRAWBERRY OLD FASHIONED

This is a non-alcoholic variation of a cocktail we serve in our speakeasy, The Office (the alcoholic version appears on page 394 of *The Aviary Cocktail Book*). Both versions feature a delicious syrup made from strawberry juice, which we clarify with the use of a specialty enzyme called Pectinex. This optional step helps yield a perfectly clear cocktail.

MINT TEA

- 150 g water
- 4 g Rare Tea Cellar Mint Meritage tea

In a medium saucepan, bring the water to a boil. Remove from heat. Measure 100 g of the hot water into a separate bowl, and add tea. Cover and let steep for 10 minutes. Strain the tea through a fine mesh strainer, discarding solids. Transfer the liquid to an airtight container and reserve in the refrigerator.

LAPSANG SOUCHONG TEA

- 150 g water
- 4 g Rare Tea Cellar Forbidden Forest Lapsang Souchong

In a medium saucepan, bring the water to a boil. Remove from heat. Measure 100 g of water into a separate bowl, and add tea. Cover and let steep for 3 minutes. Strain the tea through a fine mesh strainer, discarding solids. Transfer the liquid to an airtight container and reserve in the refrigerator.

STRAWBERRY SYRUP

- 300 g whole fresh strawberries, tops removed
- 5 drops Pectinex Ultra SP-L *(optional)*
- 125 g sugar

Juice the strawberries with a juicer. Strain the juice through a fine mesh strainer, discarding any solids.

If using Pectinex to clarify syrup:
Stir in the Pectinex and transfer the mixture to an airtight container. Reserve in the refrigerator overnight to allow solids to separate. The following day, gently scoop off any floating solids, and strain the clarified juice through a coffee filter.

Combine 125 g of the strawberry juice with sugar, whisking to dissolve the sugar completely. Reserve in an airtight container in the refrigerator.

OLD FASHIONED BATCH

- 480 g Seedlip Spice 94
- 216 g strawberry syrup
- 76 g lapsang souchong tea
- 36 g mint tea
- 32 g demerara syrup *(page 22)*
- 24 g Fee Brothers Black Walnut Bitters *(see note on page 69)*

Combine all ingredients in a medium bowl, stirring to mix thoroughly. Transfer to an airtight container and reserve in the refrigerator to chill thoroughly.

TO PORTION AND SERVE

- 1 orange peel, removed with a peeler

Place a large chunk of ice into a medium serving glass. Add 4 oz (120 ml) of the chilled cocktail batch, stirring briefly to chill. Express the orange peel over the cocktail, then insert it into the glass. Serve.

THAI PEANUT SAUCE

PEANUT STOCK

- 400 g water
- 40 g Huilerie Beaujolaise Virgin Grilled Peanut Oil

If you have sous vide equipment:
Combine all ingredients in a vacuum bag and seal. Cook en sous vide at 77°C (170°F) for at least 1 hour. Meanwhile, prepare an ice bath. Transfer the bag to the ice bath to chill completely.

If you don't have sous vide equipment:
Bring a large pot of water to a simmer. Combine all ingredients and seal in a heavy-duty zip-top bag, trying to remove as much air as possible before closing. Dip the bag into the simmering water, taking care to keep it off the bottom of the pot so the plastic doesn't burn (you can clip it to the side of the pot using a clothespin to help with this). Simmer the bag for about 1 hour. Meanwhile, prepare an ice bath. Transfer the bag to the ice bath to chill completely.

Holding the bag by one of its topmost corners over a clean bowl, use a pair of scissors to snip a small slit in the bottom-most corner, allowing the water to drain from the bottom of the bag. Pinch the slit closed just before the oil begins to drain. Discard bag and oil. Transfer the infused liquid to an airtight container and reserve.

LIME PEEL STOCK

- 150 g water
- 123 g lime peel (from about 9 large limes), removed with a peeler

Combine the water and the lime peels in a blender, and blend on high speed for 30 seconds. Strain the mixture through a fine mesh strainer, discarding solids. Transfer to an airtight container and allow to sit in the refrigerator for several hours; solids will settle to the bottom of the container. Pour off the liquid into a clean container, leaving as much sediment behind as possible. Reserve in an airtight container in the refrigerator.

THAI PEANUT SAUCE BATCH

- 325 g peanut stock
- 115 g water
- 70 g yuzu juice
- 50 g Seedlip Garden 108
- 40 g fresh ginger juice, extracted with a juicer
- 40 g sugar
- 7 g lime peel stock
- 7 g coconut palm sugar
- 1.5 g citric acid
- 1.5 g kosher salt

Combine all ingredients in a mixing bowl, whisking to dissolve sugar, acid, and salt. Transfer to an airtight container and reserve in the refrigerator to chill thoroughly.

TO PORTION AND SERVE

Pour 3 oz (90 ml) of the chilled cocktail batch into a medium serving glass. Serve.

CELERY SERRANO

The bright, springtime, green vegetable flavors in this cocktail gain an extra dimension with our inclusion of serrano pepper ice – the slower the drink is consumed, the spicier it gets.

GINGER SYRUP

- 1 large hand ginger
- 60 g sugar

Peel the ginger and slice thinly against the fibers. Extract juice from ginger using a juicer. Strain the juice through a fine mesh strainer, discarding solids. Let the juice sit for 1 hour to allow the starch to settle. Pour off the juice into a clean container, leaving as much starch behind as possible. Discard the starch.

Combine 60 g of the ginger juice with the sugar in a blender. Blend on high speed until the sugar is completely dissolved. Transfer to a glass bottle and reserve in the refrigerator. Reserve the remaining ginger juice to make serrano ice.

CELERY STOCK

- 1 head celery
- 80 g sugar *(estimated)*

Prepare an ice bath. Fill a large pot with water, and bring to a boil over high heat. Blanch the greenest celery stalks in the boiling water for 1 minute. Transfer to the ice bath to cool completely. Drain on several layers of paper towels. Extract juice from the celery using a juicer. Strain the juice through a fine mesh strainer into a clean bowl set on a scale, noting the weight. Add 25% by weight sugar (about 80 g) and whisk to dissolve completely. Transfer to an airtight container and reserve in the refrigerator.

Celery Serrano, continued

SERRANO ICE

270 g water
120 g fresh green bell pepper juice, extracted with a juicer
72 g glucose
60 g simple syrup *(page 22)*
51 g fresh serrano pepper juice, extracted with a juicer
12 g fresh ginger juice, extracted with a juicer
0.5 g salt

Combine all ingredients in a medium bowl, whisking to dissolve the glucose and salt. Strain the mixture through a fine mesh strainer. Fill a 1¼ inch (3.2 cm) square ice mold with the mixture. Freeze until completely solid. Reserve.

TO ASSEMBLE AND SERVE

2 oz (60 ml) Seedlip Garden 108
1 oz (30 ml) celery stock
¾ oz (22.5 ml) fresh lime juice
¼ oz (7.5 ml) ginger syrup

Place 2 serrano ice cubes into a medium glass.

If you have a Perlini cocktail shaker:
Combine all ingredients with ice in a Perlini shaker. Shake vigorously until chilled and diluted. Invert the shaker and charge with CO_2 until the shaker is fully-pressurized and no more gas flows in. Shake the canister to dissolve gas. Allow the contents to settle for 30 seconds, then gently vent excess gas from the canister. Pour the carbonated cocktail over the serrano ice. Serve.

If you have a carbonation device:
Combine all ingredients with ice in a cocktail shaker. Shake vigorously until chilled and diluted. Double-strain into a carbonation device. Carbonate according to manufacturer's instructions, then gently pour the carbonated cocktail over the serrano ice. Serve.

If you do not have carbonation equipment:
Combine all ingredients with ice in a cocktail shaker. Shake vigorously until chilled and diluted. Double-strain into the serving glass over the serrano ice. Serve.

Celery Serrano, continued

INSTANT OATMEAL

SALT SOLUTION

100 g hot water

3 g kosher salt

Combine the water and salt in a small bowl, whisking to completely dissolve the salt. Transfer to an airtight container and reserve.

TOASTED OATS

125 g rolled oats

Heat oven to 350°F (180°C). Spread the oats on a sheet tray and toast in the oven, stirring frequently, for about 20 minutes, or until golden brown and fragrant. Allow to cool. Reserve.

OATED VERJUS

75 g toasted oats

600 g verjus rouge

Combine the toasted oats and verjus in a blender, and blend on high speed for 5 seconds. Transfer to a large container. Allow to infuse for 24 hours; solids will settle to the bottom of the container. Gently pour the infused verjus from the container, taking care not to disturb the solids and leaving as much of them behind as possible. Discard solids. Transfer to an airtight container and reserve in the refrigerator.

INSTANT OATMEAL BATCH

370 g Malta Goya malt soda

250 g oated verjus

240 g Seedlip Spice 94

100 g demerara syrup *(page 22)*

50 g Maguey Sweet Sap

6 g Fee Brothers Black Walnut Bitters *(see note on page 69)*

3 g Fee Brothers Aztec Chocolate Bitters *(see note on page 69)*

3 g salt solution

Combine all ingredients in a medium bowl, stirring to mix thoroughly. Transfer to an airtight container and reserve in the refrigerator to chill thoroughly.

TO PORTION AND SERVE

Pour 4 oz (120 ml) of the chilled cocktail batch into a medium serving glass. Serve.

WATERMELON GINGER TONIC

GINGER SYRUP

- 1 large hand ginger
- 100g sugar

Peel the ginger and slice thinly against the fibers. Extract juice from ginger using a juicer. Strain the juice through a fine mesh strainer, discarding solids. Let the juice sit for 1 hour to allow the starch to settle. Pour off the juice into a clean container, leaving as much starch behind as possible. Discard the starch.

Combine 100g of the ginger juice with the sugar in a blender. Blend on high speed until the sugar is completely dissolved. Transfer to an airtight container and reserve in the refrigerator.

WATERMELON SYRUP

- 200g fresh watermelon juice, extracted with a juicer
- 100g sugar

In a small bowl, combine the watermelon juice and sugar, whisking to dissolve completely. Reserve in an airtight container in the refrigerator.

TURMERIC VINEGAR

- 125g water
- 30g cane vinegar
- 10g sugar
- 5g turmeric, chopped roughly

Combine all ingredients in a small saucepan, cover, and bring to a boil over high heat. Remove from heat and allow to steep for 20 minutes. Strain the mixture through a fine mesh strainer, discarding solids. Reserve in an airtight container in the refrigerator.

Watermelon Ginger Tonic, continued

WATERMELON BASE BATCH

| 250 g watermelon syrup
| 200 g water
| 200 g white grape juice
| 130 g turmeric vinegar
| 80 g ginger syrup
| 70 g Crodino

Combine all ingredients in a mixing bowl. Transfer to an airtight container and reserve in the refrigerator to chill thoroughly.

Watermelon Ginger Tonic, continued

TO ASSEMBLE AND SERVE

- 4 oz (120 ml) chilled watermelon base
- ½ oz (15 ml) fresh grapefruit juice
- ½ oz (15 ml) fresh lime juice
- 3 oz (90 ml) tonic water or sparkling water

Fill a tall glass three-quarters full of ice.

If you have a Perlini cocktail shaker:
Combine all ingredients with ice in a Perlini shaker. Shake vigorously until chilled and diluted. Invert the shaker and charge with CO_2 until the shaker is fully-pressurized and no more gas flows in. Shake the canister to dissolve gas. Allow the contents to settle for 30 seconds, then gently vent excess gas from the canister. Pour the carbonated cocktail into the serving glass over the ice. Serve with a straw.

If you have a carbonation device:
Combine cocktail base, grapefruit juice, and lime juice with ice in a cocktail shaker. Shake vigorously until chilled and diluted. Double-strain into a carbonation device, add tonic or sparkling water, and carbonate according to manufacturer's instructions. Gently pour the drink into the serving glass over the ice. Serve with a straw.

If you do not have carbonation equipment:
Combine cocktail base, grapefruit juice, and lime juice with ice in a cocktail shaker. Shake vigorously until chilled and diluted. Double-strain into the serving glass over the ice. Top with tonic or sparkling water. Serve with a straw.

AMERICANO

SPICED PEAR SYRUP

- 7g allspice, coarsely crushed
- 3g cinnamon sticks, coarsely crushed
- 150g water
- 100g pear juice
- 200g sugar

In a medium saucepan, toast the allspice and cinnamon over medium heat until fragrant. Add the water and bring to a boil. Remove from heat, cover, and allow to steep for 1 hour. Strain the mixture through a fine mesh strainer, discarding solids.

In a small bowl, combine 100g of the spiced water with all remaining ingredients, whisking to dissolve sugar completely. Transfer syrup to an airtight container and reserve in the refrigerator.

BITTER APÉRITIF *(Inspired by Bruto Americano)*

- 1000g water
- 50g grapefruit peel, removed with a peeler
- 20g orange peel, removed with a peeler
- 60g light corn syrup
- 35g dried peaches
- 30g sandalwood chips
- 20g dried figs
- 10g dried hibiscus flowers or hibiscus tea
- 10g vegetable glycerin
- 4g gentian root
- 3g dried chamomile flowers or pure chamomile tea
- 2g angelica root

In a large saucepan, combine the water and citrus peels, muddling gently to extract oil. Add all remaining ingredients and bring the mixture to a boil over high heat. Remove from the heat, cover, and allow to steep for 15 minutes. Strain the mixture through a fine mesh strainer, discarding solids. Transfer to an airtight container and reserve in the refrigerator.

AMERICANO BASE BATCH

- 346g bitter apéritif
- 220g Seedlip Spice 94
- 140g spiced pear syrup
- 52g POM pomegranate juice
- 35g Fee Brothers Black Walnut Bitters *(see note on page 69)*

Combine all ingredients in a medium bowl, stirring to mix thoroughly. Transfer to an airtight container and reserve in the refrigerator to chill thoroughly.

TO ASSEMBLE AND SERVE

- 1oz (30ml) sparkling water, very cold
- 3½oz (105ml) chilled americano base
- 1 orange peel, removed with a peeler

Place three small chunks of ice into a medium serving glass. Add the sparkling water, then the chilled cocktail base, stirring briefly to incorporate. Express the orange peel over the cocktail, then insert it into the glass. Serve.

SWEET CORN

Here we're expressing the flavors of a complex and delicious creamed corn soup as a beverage. To extract as much corn flavor as we can, we build a stock using the whole cob – husks and all – and build complexity with added aromatics of vanilla, fenugreek, and saffron. The result pairs well with most shellfish or crustacean dishes.

SWEET CORN BATCH

- 2 fresh ears of corn, husk included
- 3 whole vanilla beans
- 1500g water
- 404g light corn syrup
- 8g fenugreek seeds
- 6g mild yellow curry
- 3g kosher salt
- 3g citric acid
- 0.06g (a very small pinch) saffron threads
- 3 lemon peels, removed with a peeler

Remove the husks from the corn cobs and set them aside. Using a sharp knife, remove the kernels from each cob by slicing them off down the length of the cob. Chop the cob itself into 1 inch (2.5 cm) lengths.

Slice the vanilla pods lengthwise. Using the back of the knife blade, scrape the seeds from the pod.

In a large saucepan, combine the corn husks, kernels, and cob pieces, the vanilla seeds and pods, and all remaining ingredients. Bring the mixture to a boil. Lower heat to a simmer, and cook uncovered until reduced by about half. Remove from heat and allow to cool completely. Strain through a fine mesh strainer, discarding solids. Transfer to an airtight container and reserve in refrigerator to chill thoroughly.

TO PORTION AND SERVE

Pour 3oz (90ml) of the chilled cocktail batch into a medium serving glass. Serve.

SUMMER SUMMER

LEMONGRASS KAFFIR STOCK

- 700 g water
- 75 g fresh lemongrass, roughly chopped
- 30 g vegetable glycerin
- 5 whole dried kaffir lime leaves
- 30 g lime peel, removed with a peeler
- 20 g lemon peel, removed with a peeler

Combine the water, lemongrass, vegetable glycerin, and kaffir lime leaves in a blender. Pulse two or three times, just enough to break up the solids (taking care not to purée the mixture). Add the lime and lemon peels and muddle to combine. Transfer the mixture to an airtight container and allow to steep overnight in the refrigerator. Strain the mixture through a fine mesh strainer, discarding solids. Reserve.

LAVENDER WATERMELON ICE

- 275 g water
- 10 g lavender buds
- 375 g fresh watermelon juice, extracted with a juicer
- 20 g sugar
- 15 g glucose
- 1.5 g citric acid

In a medium saucepan, bring the water to a simmer. Remove from heat. Measure 250 g of the hot water into a separate bowl and add the lavender buds. Cover and let steep for 5 minutes. Strain the liquid through a fine mesh strainer, discarding solids.

In a clean bowl, combine 150 g of the lavender liquid with the remaining ingredients, whisking to dissolve sugars and acid. Fill a ⅜ inch (0.95 cm) ice cube mold with the mixture and freeze until completely solid. Reserve in the freezer.

Summer Summer, continued

SUMMER SUMMER BATCH

- 600g lemongrass kaffir stock
- 100g verjus blanc
- 60g Seedlip Garden 108
- 50g sugar
- 1.5g malic acid
- 1g citric acid
- 0.5g kosher salt

Combine all ingredients in a mixing bowl, whisking to dissolve the sugar, acids, and salt. Transfer to an airtight container and reserve in the refrigerator to chill thoroughly.

LEMONGRASS STRAWS

- 8–12 stalks lemongrass

Cut off the bottom end of the lemongrass, and trim the stalk to a length that is a few inches taller than your serving glass. Working from the bulb end of the stalk, use a chopstick or other long, slender utensil to carefully push the central layers of the lemongrass up and out, leaving a hollow core. Remove the outermost leaves from the stalk. Reserve straws between two damp paper towels in an airtight container in the refrigerator.

Summer Summer, continued

TO ASSEMBLE AND SERVE

4 oz (120 ml) chilled summer summer batch
½ oz (15 ml) water

Fill a medium serving glass three-quarters full of lavender watermelon ice cubes.

If you have a Perlini cocktail shaker:
Combine all ingredients with ice in a Perlini shaker. Shake vigorously until chilled and diluted. Invert the shaker and charge with CO_2 until the shaker is fully-pressurized and no more gas flows in. Shake the canister to dissolve gas. Allow the contents to settle for 30 seconds, then gently vent excess gas from the canister. Pour the carbonated cocktail into the serving glass over the ice. Serve.

If you have a carbonation device:
Combine all ingredients with ice in a cocktail shaker. Shake vigorously until chilled and diluted. Double-strain into a carbonation device and carbonate according to manufacturer's instructions. Gently pour the drink into the serving glass over the ice. Serve.

If you do not have carbonation equipment:
Combine all ingredients with ice in a cocktail shaker. Shake vigorously until chilled and diluted. Double-strain into the serving glass over the ice. Serve.

PRETZEL

The distinctive flavor of a freshly-baked soft pretzel is due in part to the deep browning its outer surface undergoes as it cooks. This browning – caused by the Maillard reaction – is made possible by a quick dip of the dough in an alkaline solution containing baking soda or lye. This solution accelerates the flavorful browning of the pretzel's outer crust.

We can replicate this process in liquid form by pressure cooking butternut squash in a solution of baking soda and using the resulting liquid as a base for our beverage. The increased temperatures provided by pressure cooking in conjunction with the baking soda help caramelize the squash, leading to flavors reminiscent of a pretzel or a bagel. We balance these with sweetness from malt soda and acidity from tart cherry juice.

This beverage was originally served as a wine, which we paired with a few umami-rich dishes featuring scallops and sausage. In this form, the drink is highly unusual and surprising. But when chilled and carbonated, it strongly resembles a dark porter-style beer in both flavor and visual presentation.

BUTTERNUT SQUASH STOCK

- 430 g butternut squash, peel removed, cut into 1 inch (2.5 cm) cubes
- 430 g water
- 7 g cacao nibs
- 5 g baking soda
- 3 g kosher salt

Combine all ingredients in a pressure cooker. Pressure cook at 15 psi for 10 minutes. Remove from heat and allow to cool completely. Strain the mixture through a fine mesh strainer, taking care not to break up the squash pieces. Discard the solids. Transfer the liquid to an airtight container and reserve in the refrigerator.

MALT SODA REDUCTION

- 300 g Malta Goya malt soda
- ¼ vanilla bean, split and scraped *(see page 21)*

Combine the soda and vanilla in a small saucepan, and bring to a boil over high heat. Reduce heat and simmer until reduced by half. Cover and allow to cool completely. Strain the mixture through a fine mesh strainer, discarding solids. Transfer the liquid to an airtight container and reserve in the refrigerator.

PRETZEL BATCH

- 390 g butternut squash stock
- 260 g tart cherry juice
- 130 g malt soda reduction
- 20 g water

Combine all ingredients in a mixing bowl. Transfer to an airtight container and reserve in the refrigerator to chill thoroughly.

TO ASSEMBLE AND SERVE

If serving carbonated:
Pour the chilled mixture into a carbonation device and carbonate according to manufacturer's instructions. Gently pour the drink into a medium serving glass. Serve.

If serving uncarbonated:
Pour 3 oz (90 ml) of the chilled batch into a small serving glass. Serve.

PECHUGA

This recipe draws inspiration from *pechuga* – a style of mezcal produced by suspending a chicken breast, along with seasonal fruits and grains, over simmering agave distillate. Produced in tiny batches for the personal consumption of the distillers and their families, the product is astoundingly complex. Delicious on its own, this drink also pairs well – perhaps unsurprisingly – with Mexican dishes.

CHICKEN BROTH *(Optional)*

Spread the bones and scraps from a whole roasted chicken onto a cookie sheet or sheet tray, and roast in an oven at 400°F (205°C) until very brown. Transfer these to a large pot and add water to cover. Bring to a boil, then lower the heat to maintain a slow simmer for around 2 hours, using a ladle or large spoon to skim away any impurities that rise to the surface.

Strain the liquid, discarding solids. Return the liquid to the heat, bring to a boil, and cook until the liquid has reduced by about half. Chill the stock in an ice bath to cool it completely, then transfer it to a large airtight container and reserve in the refrigerator.

SMOKED ICE WINE TEA

- 275g water
- 10g Rare Tea Cellar Black Canadian Smoked Ice Wine Elixir

In a medium saucepan, bring the water to a simmer. Remove from heat, and measure 250g of the hot water into a heatproof bowl. Add the tea, cover, and let steep for 6 minutes. Strain the tea through a fine mesh strainer, discarding solids. Transfer the liquid to an airtight container and reserve.

CORIANDER STOCK

- 14g coriander seeds
- 200g water
- 1g red pepper flakes

In a medium saucepan, toast the coriander over medium heat until fragrant. Add the remaining ingredients and bring to a boil, stirring constantly. Remove from heat and allow to steep for 6 minutes. Strain the mixture through a fine mesh strainer, discarding solids. Transfer the liquid to an airtight container and reserve.

PECHUGA BASE BATCH

- 200g smoked ice wine tea
- 200g agave syrup
- 150g coriander stock
- 100g homemade chicken broth, or store-bought low-sodium chicken stock
- 1.5g malic acid

Combine all ingredients in a mixing bowl, whisking to dissolve acid. Transfer to an airtight container and reserve in the refrigerator.

TO ASSEMBLE AND SERVE

- 1½oz (45ml) pechuga base
- 1½oz (45ml) fresh pineapple juice, extracted with a juicer

Combine the cocktail base and the pineapple juice with ice in a cocktail shaker. Shake briefly, then double-strain into a medium serving glass. Serve.

BRAMBLIN' MAN

This recipe was developed to pair with a dish of slow-roasted lamb, and it was originally expressed in the form of a wine. While it worked well in that context, we've re-balanced it here to be served at colder temperatures, where it can be presented as a cocktail.

BLACKBERRY POMEGRANATE SYRUP

- 440 g POM pomegranate juice
- 200 g fresh blackberries
- 37 g pomegranate molasses

Combine all ingredients in a small saucepan, cover, and bring to a boil over high heat. Remove from heat and allow to steep for 20 minutes. Strain the mixture through a fine mesh strainer, pressing on solids to extract as much juice as possible. Discard solids. Reserve.

BRAMBLIN' MAN BATCH

- 500 g blackberry pomegranate syrup
- 250 g water
- 90 g root beer
- 30 g demerara sugar

Combine all ingredients in a mixing bowl, whisking to mix thoroughly. Transfer to an airtight container and reserve in the refrigerator.

TO PORTION AND SERVE

- 1 orange peel, removed with a peeler

Place a large chunk of ice into a medium serving glass. Add 4 oz (120 ml) of the cocktail batch, stirring briefly to chill. Express the orange peel over the cocktail, then insert it into the glass. Serve.

GREEN PAPAYA SALAD

Green papaya salad – or *som tam* in Thailand – is a spicy combination of unripe papaya, lime juice, salty fish sauce, and sweet palm sugar. One of our early menus at Next exclusively featured dishes exploring the flavors of Thailand, and the profile of green papaya salad struck us as interesting to present as a drink.

When juicing papaya, we notice that the seeds impart a spicy, horseradish-like flavor to the liquid. This inspired us to swap the chili traditionally used in *som tam* for horseradish to help bolster this flavor. The spicy heat from this handily stands in for the caustic burn of alcohol, resulting in a drink that's complex yet refreshing.

GREEN PAPAYA SALAD BASE BATCH

- 1 green papaya
- 222g water
- 61g palm sugar
- 10g fresh horseradish, peeled and grated
- 9g peanut butter
- 6g lime peel, removed with a peeler
- 1.5g citric acid
- 222g water
- 156g verjus blanc
- 56g fresh pineapple juice, extracted with a juicer
- 9g fish sauce
- 0.5g kosher salt

Peel the papaya and cut it into small pieces. Juice the papaya pieces, including the seeds. Strain the juice through a fine mesh strainer, discarding solids. Set the juice aside for a moment.

Combine 222g water, palm sugar, horseradish, peanut butter, lime peel, and citric acid in a blender. Blend on high speed for 30 seconds. Strain this mixture through a fine mesh strainer, discarding solids.

Add 222g additional water, 90g of the reserved papaya juice, and all remaining ingredients, whisking to dissolve salt. Transfer the liquid to an airtight container and reserve.

TO ASSEMBLE AND SERVE

- 4oz (120ml) green papaya salad base
- ¼oz (7.5ml) fresh lime juice
- ¼oz (7.5ml) simple syrup *(page 22)*
- 4–8 large fresh mint leaves
- 1 egg white
- 1 grapefruit peel, removed with a peeler

Combine the cocktail base, lime juice, simple syrup, mint leaves, and egg white in a cocktail shaker. Dry shake until frothy. Add ice and shake again vigorously until chilled and diluted, then double-strain into a serving glass. Express the grapefruit peel over the glass, then discard the peel. Garnish with a mint leaf and a thin slice of red chili pepper. Serve.

SELF-CARBONATING CINNAMON PASSIONFRUIT FIZZ

Nearly everyone is familiar with the grade-school science fair project involving an "erupting" volcano made from vinegar and baking soda: mix an acid with a base and you get fizz. We wondered if we could use this simple principle to make a soda that could be carbonated right in front of a guest at the table. What we came up with is a surprising and tasty combination of bright, floral passionfruit and spicy cinnamon, but this simple technique can be used with endless combinations of flavors.

BLACK RICE STOCK

- 175 g Chinese black rice
- 1000 g water
- 12.5 g baking soda

Combine the rice and water in a large container, cover, and allow to soak overnight. The following day, strain the mixture through a fine mesh strainer, discarding the rice.

In a clean container, combine 500 g of the black rice water with baking soda, whisking to dissolve. Transfer to an airtight container and reserve in the refrigerator to chill thoroughly.

CINNAMON STOCK

- 17 g cinnamon sticks, coarsely crushed
- 170 g water

In a medium saucepan, toast the cinnamon over medium heat until fragrant. Add water and bring to a boil. Remove from heat and allow to steep for 20 minutes. Strain the mixture through a fine mesh strainer, discarding solids. Transfer to an airtight container and reserve.

PASSIONFRUIT COCKTAIL

- 80 g sugar
- 70 g cinnamon stock
- 50 g passionfruit purée
- 7.5 g citric acid

Combine all ingredients in a mixing bowl, whisking to dissolve sugar and acid. Transfer to an airtight container and reserve in the refrigerator to chill thoroughly.

TO ASSEMBLE AND SERVE

Pour 1oz (30 ml) of the passionfruit cocktail into a medium serving glass. Pour an equal amount of the black rice stock into a small carafe. At the table, present the guest with both vessels, then pour the black rice mixture into the passionfruit mixture to carbonate it *à la minute*.

SNAP PEA

SNAP PEA SYRUP

200 g snap peas
100 g sugar

Extract juice from the snap peas using a juicer. In a medium bowl, whisk together 100 g of the snap pea juice with sugar until completely dissolved. Transfer to an airtight container and reserve in the refrigerator to chill thoroughly.

PEACH SYRUP

100 g peach nectar
100 g sugar

In a medium bowl, whisk together the peach nectar and sugar until completely dissolved. Transfer to an airtight container and reserve in the refrigerator to chill thoroughly.

JASMINE STOCK

150 g water
4 g jasmine tea

In a medium saucepan, bring the water to a boil. Remove from heat. Measure 100 g of the hot water into a separate bowl and add the tea. Cover and let steep for 3 minutes. Strain the mixture through a fine mesh strainer, discarding solids. Transfer the liquid to a small bottle fitted with a dropper and reserve in the refrigerator to chill thoroughly.

SNAP PEA BASE BATCH

525 g Seedlip Garden 108
175 g peach syrup
4 g citric acid
8 drops jasmine stock

Combine all ingredients in a mixing bowl, whisking to dissolve acid. Transfer to an airtight container and reserve in the refrigerator to chill thoroughly.

TO ASSEMBLE AND SERVE

2½ oz (75 ml) chilled snap pea base
½ oz (15 ml) snap pea syrup
1 oz (30 ml) sparkling water, very cold

Combine snap pea base and snap pea syrup with ice in a cocktail shaker. Throw the cocktail *(see page 21)* 4–5 times to chill and aerate it, then pour it into a tall, narrow champagne flute. Gently add the sparkling water. Garnish with 2–3 drops jasmine stock. Serve.

SALTED CARAMEL CHERRY

Salted caramel and cherries are a classically delicious topping for vanilla ice cream. Here we're simply re-articulating those flavors in the form of a cocktail. We've balanced the drink to be enjoyed on its own, but the flavors work well with sweet desserts (though you may wish to adjust the seasoning accordingly).

CARAMEL PU-ERH TEA

- 150g water
- 4g Rare Tea Cellar Caramel Dream Pu-erh tea

In a medium saucepan, bring the water to a boil. Remove from heat. Measure 100g of the hot water into a heatproof bowl. Add the tea, cover, and let steep for 8 minutes. Strain the tea through a fine mesh strainer, discarding solids. Transfer the liquid to an airtight container and reserve.

TAMARIND STOCK

- 50g tamarind
- 300g water

Place the tamarind in a medium heatproof bowl. In a medium saucepan, bring the water to a boil. Remove from heat, and pour 250g of the hot water over the tamarind, stirring briefly to break up tamarind pieces. Cover the bowl and allow to steep until completely cool. Strain the mixture through a fine mesh strainer, discarding solids. Transfer the liquid to an airtight container and reserve in the refrigerator.

SALTED CARAMEL CHERRY BATCH

- 346g water
- 192g tamarind stock
- 65g maple syrup
- 34g caramel pu-erh tea
- 11g tart cherry juice
- 11g sugar
- 3.5g Fee Brothers Black Walnut Bitters *(see note on page 69)*
- 3.5g maple vinegar
- 2g kosher salt

Combine all ingredients in a mixing bowl, whisking to dissolve sugar and salt. Transfer to an airtight container and reserve in refrigerator to chill thoroughly.

TO PORTION AND SERVE

Pour 3oz (90ml) of the chilled cocktail batch into a medium serving glass. Garnish with a fresh cherry. Serve.

LOVELY BUNCH

MODERN COCKTAILS

Similar to *Return of the Mac* (page 88), here we are experimenting with the idea of evolving the flavors of a drink over time. While the Porthole vessel used in *Return of the Mac* offers a beautiful window into this transformation process, it is not strictly necessary as a tool. Other vessels – such as a teapot or a French coffee press – work equally well to this end.

CURRY BLOOD ORANGES

| 1 blood orange
| 30 g French curry (vadouvan)

Slice the blood orange into wheels about ⅛ inch (3 mm) thick. Place the curry powder in a fine mesh strainer or a sifter, and dust each blood orange wheel with the powder.

To dehydrate using a dehydrator:
Arrange the blood orange slices on a dehydrator tray. Dehydrate at 135°F (60°C) for 12 hours, or until the slices are dry. Reserve in an airtight container.

To dehydrate using a conventional oven:
Preheat an oven to 170°F (75°C), or to its lowest setting. Line a sheet tray or cookie sheet with parchment. Arrange the blood orange slices on the parchment and transfer to the oven. Dehydrate for 1 hour, then check slices every 20 minutes or so, removing slices as they become dry. Reserve the slices in an airtight container.

Lovely Bunch, continued

ROASTED BANANA PEEL

3 bananas

Preheat an oven to 350°F (175°C). Line a sheet tray with a silicone baking mat. Using a sharp knife, cut several small slits into each unpeeled banana. Transfer to prepared sheet tray. Roast the bananas for 25 minutes, or until peels turn black. Let cool completely. Remove and reserve the peels. Reserve the roasted banana fruit for another use.

LOVELY BUNCH BASE

350 g Seedlip Spice 94
175 g roasted banana peel
175 g verjus blanc
162 g water
87 g sugar
0.5 g salt

If you have sous vide equipment:
Combine all ingredients in a vacuum bag and seal. Cook en sous vide at 85°C (185°F) for at least 1 hour. Meanwhile, prepare an ice bath. Transfer the bag to the ice bath to chill completely. Strain the mixture through a fine mesh strainer, discarding solids. Transfer the strained liquid to an airtight container and reserve in refrigerator.

If you don't have sous vide equipment:
Bring a large pot of water to a simmer. Combine all ingredients and seal in a heavy-duty zip-top bag, trying to remove as much air as possible before closing. Dip the bag into the simmering water, taking care to keep it off the bottom of the pot so the plastic doesn't burn (you can clip it to the side of the pot using a clothespin to help with this). Simmer the bag for about 1 hour. Meanwhile, prepare an ice bath. Transfer the bag to the ice bath to chill completely. Strain the mixture through a fine mesh strainer, discarding solids. Transfer the strained liquid to an airtight container and reserve in refrigerator.

IN THE INFUSION VESSEL

9 g Rare Tea Cellar Wild Banana Chai
8 g dried banana chips
1 dried Ancho chile
1 curry blood orange wheel
1 cinnamon stick
1 lemon peel, removed with a channel peeler

Arrange all ingredients in an infusion vessel – such as a French press or a teapot – working from the largest ingredient to the smallest.

TO ASSEMBLE AND SERVE

Fill the infusion vessel with the chilled cocktail base. Serve with a small tasting glass. At the table, invite the guest to refill the tasting glass from infuser periodically.

ME & YOU

We love playing with the idea of presenting savory flavors in sweet dishes (and vice versa) – the surprising violation of expectations is often fun and memorable. Here we're balancing the salty, umami-rich flavor of miso with the sweetness of honey and the bright, floral acidity of yuzu. The result is unusual, yet pleasantly tasty.

MISO STOCK

- 450g water
- 20g red miso paste

In a medium saucepan, bring the water to a boil over high heat. Remove from heat and whisk in the miso until thoroughly incorporated. Cover and allow to cool completely; the miso should separate and settle to the bottom of the pot. Carefully pour the clarified liquid into a clean airtight container and reserve in the refrigerator.

ME & YOU BATCH

- 320g miso stock
- 82g honey
- 74g Concord grape juice
- 74g verjus rouge
- 25g yuzu juice
- 1g kosher salt

Combine all ingredients in a mixing bowl, whisking to dissolve salt. Transfer to an airtight container and reserve in the refrigerator.

TO ASSEMBLE AND SERVE

Combine 3oz (90ml) of the chilled cocktail batch with ice in a cocktail shaker. Shake until chilled and diluted, then double-strain into a medium glass. Serve.

IPA

India Pale Ales, or "IPAs", get their distinctive aroma from hop flowers – green conical blossoms that grow in bunches on long, wiry vines. These flowers are often infused into the beer in a process known as "dry hopping". The hops impart powerfully aromatic qualities into the beer that often resemble those of tropical fruits.

Here we are toying with the idea of articulating these qualities in cocktail form. We first build an infusion using hop flowers (available from any homebrew supply store; we use Citra hops here, but other aromatic varietals such as Cascade or Nelson Sauvin would be well worth experimenting with). We then combine this with some tropical fruit purées, and clarify this mixture using a technique often referred to as "gelatin clarification".

HOP STOCK

500g water
30g Citra hops

If you have sous vide equipment:
Combine the water and hops in a vacuum bag and seal. Cook en sous vide at 70°C (160°F) for at least 30 minutes. Meanwhile, prepare an ice bath. Transfer the bag to the ice bath to chill completely. Strain the mixture through a fine mesh strainer, discarding solids. Transfer to an airtight container and reserve in the refrigerator.

If you don't have sous vide equipment:
Bring a medium pot of water to a simmer. Combine the water and hops in a metal non-reactive mixing bowl, and cover tightly with plastic wrap. Set this bowl over the simmering water, and heat for 30 minutes. Meanwhile, prepare an ice bath. Float the covered bowl in the ice bath to chill completely. Strain the mixture through a fine mesh strainer, discarding solids. Transfer to an airtight container and reserve in the refrigerator.

IPA, continued

CLARIFIED PASSIONFRUIT MANGO STOCK

- 5 sheets gelatin
- 390g passionfruit purée
- 390g mango purée
- 390g hop stock

Immerse the gelatin sheets in ice water for 5 minutes, or until pliable. Gather the gelatin, squeeze out water, and reserve.

Combine the fruit purées and hop stock in a large mixing bowl. Weigh 100g of this mixture into a small saucepan, and warm gently over medium-low heat. Add the gelatin and stir until dissolved. Combine this mixture with the remaining purée, stirring to mix thoroughly.

Line a sheet tray or a baking dish with plastic wrap. Transfer the purée mixture to this container and freeze overnight. The following day, remove the frozen purée from the freezer, invert it onto 3 layers of cheesecloth, and wrap tightly. Place the wrapped frozen purée onto a wire rack above a sheet tray, and let drip for 12–14 hours at room temperature. Gently transfer the clarified stock to an airtight container. Reserve in the refrigerator.

IPA BATCH

- 375g water
- 300g clarified passionfruit mango stock
- 45g sugar
- 1g kosher salt
- 0.5g citric acid

Combine all ingredients in a mixing bowl, whisking to dissolve sugar, salt, and acid. Transfer to an airtight container and reserve in the refrigerator to chill thoroughly.

TO PORTION AND SERVE

Pour 3oz (90ml) of the chilled cocktail batch into a medium serving glass. Serve.

IPA, continued

RHUBARB, THYME, JUNIPER

MODERN COCKTAILS

THYME SIMPLE SYRUP

- 150 g sugar
- 150 g hot water
- 38 g fresh thyme

Combine the sugar and water in a small bowl, whisking to completely dissolve sugar. Allow the mixture to cool completely, then add the thyme and muddle gently. Transfer to an airtight container and allow to steep for 48 hours in the refrigerator. Strain the mixture through a fine mesh strainer, discarding solids. Transfer to an airtight container and reserve in the refrigerator.

SALT SOLUTION

- 100 g hot water
- 3 g kosher salt

Combine the water and salt in a small bowl, whisking to completely dissolve salt. Transfer to an airtight container and reserve.

CLARIFIED RHUBARB JUICE

- 400 g rhubarb

Chop rhubarb into small pieces and extract juice with a juicer. Strain the juice through a fine mesh strainer, discarding solids. Transfer to a tall airtight container and reserve in the refrigerator overnight to allow fine particles to settle. Gently pour the clarified liquid into a clean container, taking care not to disturb sediment. Reserve in the refrigerator.

RHUBARB, THYME, JUNIPER BATCH

- 380 g gin (from page 28)
- 185 g thyme simple syrup
- 150 g clarified rhubarb juice
- 100 g verjus rouge
- 1.5 g salt solution

Combine all ingredients in a mixing bowl. Transfer to an airtight container and reserve in the refrigerator to chill thoroughly.

TO PORTION AND SERVE

- 3 oz (90 ml) chilled rhubarb, thyme, juniper batch

Fill a medium serving glass halfway with ice. Add the chilled cocktail batch. Garnish with a small sprig of thyme. Serve with a straw.

MOLE

Mole (pronounced, in this context, "mole-ay") is a traditional sauce found in Mexican cuisine. It is a rich, complex concoction generally built with fruit, chili pepper, nuts, and copious spices, and it is usually served as an accompaniment to meat.

Here we're re-articulating the flavors and preparation into the format of a cocktail. We adjust the consistency of the sauce to be pleasant when sipped, and balance it with acidity and sweetness so that it can stand on its own as a beverage. While satisfying on its own, this cocktail shines when paired – obviously – with Mexican food.

MOLE BATCH

- 8g cinnamon sticks, coarsely crushed
- 7g black sesame seeds
- 10 whole black peppercorns
- 185g prune juice
- 173g raisins
- 143g verjus rouge
- 124g blackberries
- 82g light brown sugar
- 47g unsalted roasted peanuts
- 33g molasses
- 18g walnuts
- 11g dried ancho chiles, seeds and stems removed
- 4g dried guajillo chiles, seeds and stems removed
- 4g cacao nibs
- 5 whole cloves
- 550g water

In a large saucepan, toast the cinnamon, sesame, and black peppercorns over medium heat until fragrant. Add all remaining ingredients and bring to a boil, stirring constantly. Transfer the mixture to a food processor (working in batches if necessary) and pulse once or twice to break up solids. Cover and allow to cool completely. Strain the mixture through a fine mesh strainer, discarding solids. Transfer the liquid to an airtight container and reserve in the refrigerator to chill thoroughly.

TO PORTION AND SERVE

- 1 lime peel, removed with a peeler

Pour 3oz (90ml) of the chilled cocktail batch into a medium serving glass. Express the lime peel over the drink, then garnish the drink with the peel. Serve.

BACK BAR

CLASSIC
COCKTAILS

MODERN
COCKTAILS

Chapter Four
WINES

ETCETERA

WINES

The experience of drinking wine is notably different than that of cocktails. Some wines may be served chilled (though usually not to the same icy temperatures of most cocktails); others are served at warmer temperatures. Whereas the character of alcohol in cocktails is assertive, it tends to play a softer role in wines, allowing more room for complex, organic flavors. The world of wines offers us new inspiration for exploration.

Our own experimentation with alcohol-free, wine-like beverages stems directly from the fact that we offer wine pairings with the meals we serve at some of our restaurants. We want to offer guests who prefer not to drink alcohol a beverage pairing experience that not only harmonizes perfectly with their meal, but with the experience of other (wine-drinking) guests at the table. If we offer three guests at the table an opulent Barolo to pair with a given course, presenting a fourth non-drinking guest with a brightly-colored cocktail would be jarringly dissonant for everyone.

As with cocktails, sometimes we design recipes to directly mimic a particular wine, while in other cases we completely depart from any obvious oenological touchpoint. Rather than considering wines as a constraint, we view them as an extension to our beverage design repertoire. Indeed, with appropriate adjustments to sweetness, acidity, et cetera, many of the recipes in previous sections could conceivably be presented as wines rather than cocktails.

GRAPEFRUIT JICAMA CHAMPAGNE

This recipe seeks to replicate the drinking experience of a dry Champagne or sparkling wine. Grapefruit peel and juice add bright, floral, citrus notes, while the starch in jicama juice provides a slightly "grippy", tannic mouthfeel. If you prefer your mimosas on the dry side, this recipe can be substituted in the *Grapefruit Mimosa* on page 48.

GRAPEFRUIT JICAMA CHAMPAGNE BATCH

- 200g white grape juice
- 5g rose hips
- 7g fresh basil leaves
- 30g grapefruit peel, removed with vegetable peeler
- 360g water
- 60g fresh grapefruit juice
- 50g fresh jicama juice, extracted with a juicer
- 25g verjus blanc
- 1g citric acid

Fill a large bowl with ice, and set a smaller bowl inside it. In a medium saucepan, bring the grape juice to a boil over medium heat. Remove from heat, stir in rose hips, cover, and allow to steep for 10 minutes. After this time, add the basil and allow to steep for 5 additional minutes. Finally, stir in the grapefruit peels and allow to steep for an additional 5 minutes. Strain the mixture through a fine mesh strainer into the bowl set over ice, discarding solids. Allow the mixture to cool completely.

Measure 185g of the infused liquid into a medium bowl, and stir in all of the remaining ingredients. Transfer to a carbonation device, and chill thoroughly in the refrigerator or in an ice bath. Carbonate according to manufacturer's instructions. Reserve in the refrigerator.

TO PORTION AND SERVE

Gently pour 3oz (90ml) of the chilled batch into a tall, narrow champagne flute. Serve

TRUFFLED CHERRY

TRUFFLE OIL STOCK

200g water
7g black truffle oil

If you have sous vide equipment:
Combine the water and black truffle oil in a vacuum bag and seal. Cook en sous vide at 80°C (175°F) for at least 4 hours. Meanwhile, prepare an ice bath. Transfer the bag to the ice bath to chill completely.

If you don't have sous vide equipment:
Bring a large pot of water to a simmer. Combine the water and black truffle oil and seal in a heavy-duty zip-top bag, trying to remove as much air as possible before closing. Dip the bag into the simmering water, taking care to keep it off the bottom of the pot so the plastic doesn't burn (you can clip it to the side of the pot using a clothespin to help with this). Simmer the bag for about 4 hours. Meanwhile, prepare an ice bath. Transfer the bag to the ice bath to chill completely.

Holding the bag by one of its topmost corners over a clean bowl, use a pair of scissors to snip a small slit in the bottommost corner, allowing the water to drain from the bottom of the bag. Pinch the slit closed just before the oil begins to drain. Discard bag and oil. Transfer the infused liquid to an airtight container and reserve.

TRUFFLED CHERRY BATCH

215g water
215g tart cherry juice
185g truffle oil stock
80g Maguey Sweet Sap
55g bergamot purée
25g sugar
1g kosher salt

Combine all ingredients in a mixing bowl, whisking to dissolve sugar and salt. Transfer to an airtight container and reserve in the refrigerator until ready to serve.

TO PORTION AND SERVE

Allow the reserved batch to warm to room temperature, then pour 3oz (90ml) of it into a medium serving glass. Serve.

GRAPEFRUIT TURMERIC SHRUB

Vinegar can be an interesting alternative to citrus juice for adding acidity to a drink. Think of squeezing a bit of lime into a glass of water – a well-balanced shrub offers a similar taste experience with a slightly different flavor profile. This recipe and the other shrubs found in this section were each crafted to pair with food, and were designed to offer a similar drinking experience as that of an acidic white wine.

GRAPEFRUIT VINEGAR

- 100 g Silver Swan sugar cane vinegar
- 33 g fresh red grapefruit slices (including rind)
- 20 g fresh turmeric, peeled and roughly chopped
- 5 g fresh tarragon
- 0.5 g dried hibiscus flowers

If you have sous vide equipment:
Combine all ingredients in a vacuum bag and seal. Cook en sous vide at 70°C (160°F) for 4 hours. Meanwhile, prepare an ice bath. Transfer the bag to the ice bath to chill completely.

If you don't have sous vide equipment:
Bring a medium pot of water to a simmer. Combine all ingredients in a metal non-reactive mixing bowl, and cover tightly with plastic wrap. Set this bowl over the simmering water, and heat for 4 hours. Meanwhile, prepare an ice bath. Float the covered bowl in the ice bath to chill completely. Reserve the mixture in the refrigerator.

Strain the mixture through a fine mesh strainer, discarding solids. Transfer the liquid to an airtight container, cover, and allow it to cool completely. Reserve in the refrigerator.

GRAPEFRUIT TURMERIC SHRUB BATCH

- 610 g water
- 76 g grapefruit vinegar
- 49.5 g sugar
- 10.5 g vegetable glycerin
- 2 g citric acid
- 0.5 g kosher salt

Combine all ingredients in a mixing bowl, whisking to dissolve sugar and acid. Transfer to an airtight container and reserve in the refrigerator to chill thoroughly.

TO PORTION AND SERVE

Pour 3 oz (90 ml) of the chilled shrub batch into a medium serving glass. Serve.

BANANA CHAI

When warm milk is combined with acidic liquid, the milk instantly curdles. These curds, in turn, can trap and filter particles from the mixture, producing a clear liquid with an unctuous, creamy mouthfeel. A liquid clarified using this technique is often referred to as a "milk punch".

In this recipe, we use the technique to clarify a thick, full-flavored blend of bananas, chai tea, and chocolate. The mixture resembles a smoothie – both visually and in flavor – when first blended together. After the milk curds are allowed to do their work, however, we get a beautifully-clear drink that resembles a crisp white wine.

BANANA CHAI

| 800g water
| 30g Rare Tea Cellar Wild Banana Chai

In a medium saucepan, bring the water to a boil. Remove from heat. Measure 750g of the hot water into a separate bowl and add tea. Cover and let steep for 10 minutes. Strain the tea through a fine mesh strainer, discarding solids. Transfer the liquid to an airtight container and reserve.

ROASTED BANANA

| 5 bananas

Preheat an oven to 350°F (175°C). Line a sheet tray with parchment or a silicone baking mat. Using a sharp knife, cut several small slits into each unpeeled banana. Transfer to the prepared sheet tray. Roast the bananas for 25 minutes, or until their peels turn black. Remove the bananas from the oven and let them cool completely. Remove and discard peels.

Banana Chai, continued

BANANA MILK PUNCH BATCH

- 1 vanilla bean
- 600g water
- 600g banana chai
- 390g roasted banana
- 6g cocoa powder
- 5g lactic acid
- 340g milk
- 36g sugar
- 3g salt

Slice the vanilla pod lengthwise. Using the back of the knife blade, scrape the seeds from the pod. Combine the vanilla seeds and pod, water, banana chai, roasted bananas, cocoa powder, and lactic acid in a blender. Blend on high speed for 30 seconds. Transfer the mixture to a medium bowl and set aside.

In a small saucepan over medium heat, warm the milk gently just until it begins to steam (taking care not to bring it to a boil). Remove from heat and pour into the banana mixture – the milk should instantly curdle. Allow the mixture to cool, then cover and store in the refrigerator overnight, or preferably two days for a more clarified final result.

Gather two large bowls. Set a fine mesh strainer over one bowl and begin pouring the curdled milk mixture into it. The milk curds will settle into the strainer and begin to form a filtration bed. As the liquid begins to run clear, move the strainer over the second bowl and continue straining. When finished, gently pour the reserved cloudy portion from first bowl over the curds in the strainer into second bowl to further clarify it, taking care to disturb the curds as little as possible.

Combine 750g of the clarified milk punch with the sugar and salt, whisking to dissolve completely. Transfer the mixture to an airtight container. Reserve in the refrigerator to chill thoroughly.

TO PORTION AND SERVE

Pour 3oz (90ml) of the chilled batch into a medium serving glass. Serve.

Banana Chai, continued

CARDAMOM PORT

The fragrant sweetness of cardamom, subtle savoriness of sun-dried tomato, and chocolatey spice of dried chiles lead this drink to be an interesting dessert companion – it pairs especially well with rich, chocolate dishes.

CHILE CARDAMOM STOCK

- 12 g red cardamom pods, coarsely crushed
- 3 g dried Guajillo chiles, seeds and stems removed, coarsely crushed
- 300 g water
- 20 g sun-dried tomatoes, roughly chopped
- 10 g dried hibiscus flowers or hibiscus tea

In a medium saucepan, toast the cardamom pods and chiles over medium heat until fragrant. Add the remaining ingredients and bring to a boil. Remove from heat, cover, and allow to steep for 20 minutes. Strain the mixture through a fine mesh strainer, discarding solids. Reserve.

CARDAMOM PORT BATCH

- 300 g water
- 255 g chile cardamom stock
- 95 g brown sugar
- 78 g verjus rouge
- 16 g molasses

Combine all ingredients in a mixing bowl, whisking to dissolve the brown sugar and molasses. Transfer to an airtight container and reserve in the refrigerator until ready to serve.

TO PORTION AND SERVE

Pour 3 oz (90 ml) of the chilled batch into a medium serving glass. Allow the mixture to warm to room temperature, then serve.

ROOM FOR DESSERT?

Here we take some classic after-dinner dessert flavors (coffee, orange, and chocolate) and present them as an after-dinner *digestif*. The balance and mouthfeel of this drink is similar to that of a rich, viscous wine like Sauternes, which in turn encourages small portion sizes and slow sipping. While it's probably a bit sweet to be enjoyed on its own, this recipe works very well with dessert or cheese courses.

COFFEE CHICORY STOCK

- 275 g water
- 10 g coffee beans, coarsely crushed
- 5 g chicory
- 2.5 g licorice root extract
- 1 g bitter orange peel

Combine all ingredients in a medium saucepan, cover, and bring to a boil. Remove from heat and allow to steep for 20 minutes. Strain the mixture through a fine mesh strainer, discarding solids. Reserve.

WHITE CHOCOLATE SYRUP

- 200 g water
- 100 g white chocolate, coarsely chopped
- 300 g sugar

Fill a large bowl with ice, and set a smaller bowl inside of it. Bring the water to boil in a small saucepan. Remove from heat and add the white chocolate, whisking until the chocolate has melted. Transfer the mixture to bowl set over ice and allow to cool until the chocolate fat has solidified. Strain the mixture through a fine mesh strainer, discarding solids. Add sugar, whisking to dissolve completely. Transfer to a glass bottle and reserve in the refrigerator.

ROOM FOR DESSERT? BATCH

- 225 g water
- 225 g coffee chicory stock
- 150 g blood orange purée
- 150 g white chocolate syrup
- 1.5 g citric acid
- 0.5 g ascorbic acid

Combine all ingredients in a mixing bowl, whisking to dissolve acids. Transfer to an airtight container and reserve in the refrigerator to chill thoroughly.

TO PORTION AND SERVE

Pour 2 oz (60 ml) of the chilled batch into a small serving glass. Serve.

Our use of dried rose petals in this recipe introduces not only a lovely color to this champagne, but also the dry, sandpapery mouthfeel reminiscent of tannic wines. This recipe is a fun one to experiment with: by adjusting the proportions of rose stock and sugar, you can push and pull this tannic quality around to your liking. The recipe as shared here produces the result in the leftmost image, which is to say: noticeably tannic and very dry.

ROSE CHAMPAGNE

ROSE STOCK

- 450g water
- 15g Rare Tea Cellar Wild Dried Red Rose

In a medium saucepan, bring the water to a boil. Remove from heat. Measure 400g of the hot water into a separate bowl and add the rose tea. Cover and let steep for 7 minutes. Strain the tea through a fine mesh strainer, discarding solids. Transfer the liquid to an airtight container and reserve.

YEAST STOCK

- 200g water
- 5g Red Star Premier Blanc Champagne yeast

Combine the water and yeast in a small saucepan, cover, and bring to a boil. Lower heat and simmer for 5 minutes. Remove from heat and let cool completely. Strain the mixture through a fine mesh strainer, discarding solids. Reserve.

ROSE CHAMPAGNE BATCH

- 264g water
- 264g rose stock
- 100g yeast stock
- 105g verjus rouge
- 25g sugar
- 1.5g malic acid
- 0.5g kosher salt
- 5 drops kieselsol
- 5 drops chitosan

Combine the water, rose stock, yeast stock, verjus, sugar, malic acid, and salt in a mixing bowl. Stir in the kieselsol, then add the chitosan. Cover and allow the mixture to settle in the refrigerator overnight. Gently pour off the clarified liquid, leaving as much sediment as possible behind. Transfer the clarified liquid to a carbonation device, and chill thoroughly in the refrigerator or in an ice bath. Carbonate according to manufacturer's instructions. Reserve in the refrigerator.

TO PORTION AND SERVE

Gently pour 3oz (90ml) of the chilled champagne into a tall, narrow champagne flute. Serve.

SUN DRIED

We originally designed this wine-like beverage to accompany a dish of roasted butternut squash and feta. The predominant flavors are those of dried fruits including prunes, raisins, and figs. Complexity is added by the use of toasted spices, with a touch of balancing bitterness provided by citrus peel.

FIG PURÉE

- 200 g dried black mission figs
- 200 g hot water

Combine the figs and water in a blender, and blend on high speed for 1 minute, or until the purée is completely smooth, adding more hot water if necessary to keep the mixture in motion as the blender is running. Strain the mixture through a fine mesh strainer, discarding solids. Reserve.

SUN DRIED BATCH

- 1.5 g cinnamon sticks, coarsely crushed
- 1 g allspice
- 1 g Szechuan peppercorn
- 1 star anise pod
- 360 g water
- 260 g Dr. Pepper
- 120 g fig purée
- 30 g raisins
- 7 g demerara sugar
- 0.5 g citric acid
- 4 orange peels, removed with a peeler

In a medium saucepan, toast the cinnamon, allspice, Szechuan peppercorn, and star anise over medium heat until fragrant. Add the remaining ingredients and bring to a boil, stirring constantly. Remove from heat and allow to steep for 1 hour. Strain through a fine mesh strainer, discarding solids. Transfer to an airtight container and reserve in the refrigerator.

TO PORTION AND SERVE

Pour 3 oz (90 ml) of the chilled batch into a medium serving glass. Allow the mixture to warm to room temperature, then serve.

SPICED BLUEBERRY SHRUB

SMOKED ICE WINE TEA

150 g water
4 g Rare Tea Cellar Black Canadian Smoked Ice Wine Elixir

In a medium saucepan, bring the water to a simmer. Remove from heat. Measure 100 g of the hot water into a separate bowl and add the tea. Cover and let steep for 5 minutes. Strain the tea through a fine mesh strainer, discarding solids. Transfer the liquid to an airtight container and reserve.

3-SPICE VINEGAR

1.5 g star anise
1 g cinnamon sticks, coarsely crushed
65 g water
53 g apple cider vinegar
33 g black vinegar
27 g dried pear pieces
0.5 g whole Szechuan peppercorns

In a medium saucepan, toast the star anise and cinnamon pieces over medium heat until fragrant.

If you have sous vide equipment:
Combine all ingredients in a vacuum bag and seal. Cook en sous vide at 70°C (160°F) for 4 hours. Meanwhile, prepare an ice bath. Transfer the bag to the ice bath to chill completely.

If you don't have sous vide equipment:
Bring a medium pot of water to a simmer. Combine all ingredients in a metal non-reactive mixing bowl, and cover tightly with plastic wrap. Set this bowl over the simmering water, and heat for 4 hours. Meanwhile, prepare an ice bath. Float the covered bowl in the ice bath to chill completely. Reserve the mixture in the refrigerator.

Strain the mixture through a fine mesh strainer, discarding solids. Transfer the liquid to an airtight container, cover, and allow it to cool completely. Reserve in the refrigerator.

SPICED BLUEBERRY SHRUB BATCH

570 g water
90 g 3-spice vinegar
45 g smoked ice wine tea
30 g blueberry juice
25 g sugar
20 g vegetable glycerin
0.5 g malic acid

Combine all ingredients in a mixing bowl, whisking to dissolve sugar and acid. Transfer to an airtight container and reserve in the refrigerator to chill thoroughly.

TO PORTION AND SERVE

Pour 3 oz (90 ml) of the chilled shrub batch into a medium serving glass. Serve.

STRAWBERRY TOMATO

This beverage is an interesting experiment in perception, balance, and seasoning. Strawberries and vanilla are generally associated with sweetness, whereas tomato and bay leaf are often considered savory flavors. Here, these flavors stand in almost exact opposition to one another, offering a taste experience that may strike some as puzzling.

To add further interest, we can selectively "push" the drink towards one end of the sweet/savory spectrum or the other by seasoning it in different ways. A small addition of sugar tends to cause the strawberry and vanilla flavors to be perceived more predominantly, while salt pulls the tomato and bay to the foreground. This flexibility makes this wine an interesting one to pair with food.

SENCHA

- 340 g water
- 12 g Rare Tea Cellar Sencha

In a medium saucepan, bring the water to a simmer. Remove from heat. Measure 290 g of the hot water into a separate bowl and add tea. Cover and let steep for 10 minutes. Strain the tea through a fine mesh strainer, discarding solids. Transfer the liquid to an airtight container and reserve.

Strawberry Tomato, continued

STRAWBERRY TOMATO BATCH

150 g fresh strawberries, tops removed
450 g tomatoes, roughly chopped
250 g water
225 g sencha
50 g sugar
6 g citric acid
4 bay leaves
¼ vanilla bean, split and scraped
0.5 g kosher salt
220 g whole milk

Combine the strawberries, tomatoes, water, sencha, sugar, citric acid, bay leaves, vanilla, and salt in a blender. Blend on high speed for 30 seconds. Transfer the mixture to a large bowl and set aside.

In a small saucepan over medium heat, warm the milk gently just until it begins to steam, taking care not to allow it to boil. Pour the hot milk into the strawberry-tomato mixture and stir gently – the milk should instantly curdle. Allow the mixture to cool, then cover and transfer to the refrigerator overnight.

Gather two large bowls. Set a fine mesh strainer over one bowl and begin pouring the curdled milk mixture into it. The curds will settle into the strainer and begin to form a filtration bed. As the mixture begins to run clear, move the strainer over the second bowl and continue straining. When finished, gently pour the reserved cloudy portion from first bowl over the curds in the strainer into second bowl to further clarify it, taking care to disturb curds as little as possible. Discard the solids. Transfer the liquid to an airtight container and reserve in the refrigerator to chill thoroughly.

TO PORTION AND SERVE

Pour 3 oz (90 ml) of the chilled batch into a medium serving glass. Serve.

LYCHEE CHAMPAGNE

LYCHEE CHAMPAGNE BATCH

785 g (one 750 ml bottle) verjus blanc
140 g lychee purée
85 g pear juice
82 g sugar

Combine all ingredients in a mixing bowl, whisking to dissolve sugar. Transfer to a carbonation device, and chill thoroughly in the refrigerator or in an ice bath. Carbonate according to manufacturer's instructions. Reserve in the refrigerator.

TO PORTION AND SERVE

Gently pour 3 oz (90 ml) of the chilled champagne into a tall, narrow champagne flute. Serve.

PEACH SHRUB

BITTER ORANGE TINCTURE

- 10g dried bitter orange peel
- 20g vegetable glycerin
- 40g water

Combine the peel and glycerin in a small bowl, stirring to mix thoroughly. Cover and allow to steep overnight. The following day, add the water and stir to combine. Strain the mixture through a fine mesh strainer, discarding solids. Transfer to a small glass bottle or other airtight container and reserve in the refrigerator.

PEACH TEA

- 200g water
- 6.5g Rare Tea Cellar Georgia Peach Nectar Rooibos

In a medium saucepan, bring the water to a boil. Remove from heat. Measure 170g of the hot water into a separate bowl and add the tea. Cover and let steep for 7 minutes. Strain the tea through a fine mesh strainer, discarding solids. Transfer the liquid to an airtight container and reserve.

PEACH VINEGAR

- 2 fresh peaches
- 3g whole allspice berries, coarsely-crushed
- 200g Silver Swan sugar cane vinegar
- 12.5g fresh parsley

Peel the peaches and slice in half, removing pits. Slice each half into thin disks.

In a medium saucepan, toast the allspice over medium heat until fragrant.

If you have sous vide equipment:
Combine the peaches, allspice, and vinegar in a vacuum bag and seal. Cook en sous vide at 70°C (160°F) for 2 hours.

If you don't have sous vide equipment:
Bring a medium pot of water to a simmer. Combine the peaches, allspice, and vinegar in a metal non-reactive mixing bowl, and cover tightly with plastic wrap. Set this bowl over the simmering water, and heat for 2 hours.

While the vinegar is cooking, measure the parsley into a small mixing bowl. When the vinegar is done, pour the mixture over the parsley and stir or muddle briefly. Cover and allow to steep for 5–7 minutes. Strain the mixture through a fine mesh strainer, discarding solids. Transfer the liquid to an airtight container, cover, and allow it to cool completely, then reserve it in the refrigerator.

PEACH SHRUB BATCH

- 554g water
- 85g peach vinegar
- 70g sugar
- 64g peach tea
- 2g bitter orange tincture
- 1.5g malic acid
- 1g kosher salt

Combine all ingredients in a mixing bowl, whisking to dissolve sugar, acid, and salt. Transfer to an airtight container. Reserve in the refrigerator to chill thoroughly.

TO PORTION AND SERVE

Pour 3oz (90ml) of the chilled shrub batch into a medium serving glass. Serve.

BLUEBERRY PANCAKES

When discussing beverage pairings at Next, our sommelier remarked of one wine selection that it "tastes like blueberry pancakes." Moments like these often send us off in interesting creative directions, and we rarely consider anything too absurd to explore. After all, blueberry pancakes are delicious on a plate – why wouldn't those same flavors also work well in a glass?

We replicate the warm, toasty notes of the pancake itself by heavily toasting some rice, which allows us a tidier infusion than were we to literally soak bread in water (though the latter could certainly be done). While our presentation here is served warm, this recipe can easily be served chilled (and accordingly re-balanced) if the intent is to offer a more surprising drinking experience.

BROWN BUTTER STOCK

- 30 g unsalted butter
- 200 g water

Place the butter into a small saucepan, and set this over medium-high heat. Brown the butter – it will first melt, then will froth until finally taking on a nutty brown color and aroma. At this point, immediately add the water, stirring to combine.

If you have sous vide equipment:

Transfer the butter mixture to a vacuum bag and seal. Cook en sous vide at 70°C (160°F) for at least 1 hour. Meanwhile, prepare an ice bath. Transfer the bag to the ice bath to chill until the butter fat solidifies. Using sharp scissors, cut a small incision in the bottom corner of the bag. Drain the liquid contents through a coffee filter, leaving the solids behind. Transfer the strained liquid to an airtight container and reserve.

If you don't have sous vide equipment:

Transfer the butter mixture to an airtight container. Store the container in a warm location (such as on top of your refrigerator) for 1 week, shaking or stirring daily. After a week, chill the container in an ice bath until the butter has solidified. Pour off the liquid portion of the container's contents. Strain this liquid through a coffee filter. Transfer the strained liquid to a clean airtight container and reserve.

Reserve the solidified brown butter fat separately in an airtight container.

Blueberry Pancakes, continued

TOASTED RICE STOCK

- 50g jasmine rice
- 900g water

Preheat an oven to 425°F (220°C). Spread the rice onto a cookie sheet or sheet tray. Toast the rice in the oven, stirring occasionally, for about 20 minutes, or until brown and very fragrant. Remove the rice from the oven and let cool completely.

If you have sous vide equipment:
Combine the rice and water in a vacuum bag and seal. Cook en sous vide at 82°C (180°F) for at least 2 hours. Meanwhile, prepare an ice bath. Transfer the bag to the ice bath to chill completely. Strain the mixture through a fine mesh strainer, discarding solids. Transfer the strained liquid to an airtight container and reserve.

If you don't have sous vide equipment:
Bring a large pot of water to a simmer. Seal the rice and water in a heavy-duty zip-top bag, trying to remove as much air as possible before closing. Dip the bag into the simmering water, taking care to keep it off the bottom of the pot so the plastic doesn't burn (you can clip it to the side of the pot using a clothespin to help with this). Simmer the bag for about 2 hours. Meanwhile, prepare an ice bath. Transfer the bag to the ice bath to chill completely. Strain the mixture through a fine mesh strainer, discarding solids. Transfer the strained liquid to an airtight container and reserve.

Blueberry Pancakes, continued

BLUEBERRY PANCAKES BATCH

- 550g toasted rice stock
- 150g brown butter stock
- 150g blueberry juice
- 40g maple syrup
- 20g sugar
- 20g glucose
- 2g kosher salt
- 1g citric acid

Combine all ingredients in a mixing bowl, whisking to mix thoroughly. Transfer to an airtight container and reserve in the refrigerator.

TO ASSEMBLE AND SERVE

Place a small dollop (about 1 tsp) of the reserved brown butter into the bottom of a serving glass. Warm the cocktail batch gently in a microwave or on the stovetop. Pour 3oz (90ml) of the warm cocktail batch into the serving glass over the butter. Serve.

GREEN HERB SHRUB

WINES

GREEN HERB VINEGAR

- 100 g Silver Swan sugar cane vinegar
- 12.5 g fresh parsley
- 2 g fresh tarragon
- 1.5 g fresh Thai basil
- 1 g fresh thyme
- 1 g whole green peppercorns, coarsely cracked
- 1 whole green cardamom pod
- 0.5 g coriander seeds, coarsely crushed

If you have sous vide equipment:
Combine all ingredients in a vacuum bag and seal. Cook en sous vide at 70°C (160°F) for 30 minutes. Meanwhile, prepare an ice bath. Transfer the bag to the ice bath to chill completely.

If you don't have sous vide equipment:
Bring a large pot of water to a simmer. Combine all ingredients in a heavy-duty zip-top bag, trying to remove as much air as possible before sealing. Dip the bag into the simmering water, taking care to keep it off the bottom of the pot so the plastic doesn't burn (you can clip it to the side of the pot using a clothespin to help with this). Simmer the bag for 30 minutes. Meanwhile, prepare an ice bath. Transfer the bag to the ice bath to chill completely.

Strain the mixture through a fine mesh strainer, discarding solids. Transfer the liquid to an airtight container, cover, and allow it to cool completely. Reserve in the refrigerator.

GREEN HERB SHRUB BATCH

- 600 g water
- 60 g sugar
- 50 g green herb vinegar
- 1 g citric acid
- 0.1 g (a very small pinch) kosher salt

Combine all ingredients in a mixing bowl, whisking to dissolve sugar and acid. Transfer to an airtight container and reserve in the refrigerator to chill thoroughly.

TO PORTION AND SERVE

Pour 3 oz (90 ml) of the chilled shrub batch into a medium serving glass. Serve.

UMAMI BOMB

This deeply earthy concoction was originally designed to pair with a dish of roasted maitake mushrooms, which themselves are often described as tasting like roast chicken. It pairs well with other umami-rich foods, though can be a bit challenging when consumed on its own.

BLACK GARLIC PURÉE

- 300g water
- 12g black garlic

Combine the water and garlic in a blender, and blend on high speed for 1 minute, or until smooth. Strain the purée through a fine mesh strainer. Reserve.

UMAMI BOMB BATCH

- 225g water
- 160g Concord grape juice
- 150g verjus rouge
- 100g black garlic purée
- 45g cane syrup
- 20g fresh beet juice, extracted with a juicer
- 14g low-sodium tamari
- 1g kosher salt

Combine all ingredients in a mixing bowl, whisking to dissolve salt. Transfer to an airtight container and reserve in the refrigerator until ready to serve.

TO PORTION AND SERVE

Allow the reserved chilled batch to warm to room temperature, then pour 3oz (90ml) of it into a medium serving glass. Serve.

BACK BAR

CLASSIC
COCKTAILS

MODERN
COCKTAILS

WINES

Chapter Five

ETCETERA

BREAKFAST STOUT

A traditional stout beer (of which Guinness is a classic example) gets its color and flavor from the use of deeply-roasted barley. The roasting imparts flavors often referred to as "coffee"- or "chocolate"-like, and brewers often combine these flavors with complementary ones such as milk sugar or actual cocoa.

Here we pair these roasted flavors with oats, raisins, and brown sugar. The addition of lactose – a non-fermentable sugar derived from milk – gives the beer a creamy, full mouthfeel (experiment with raising or lowering the amount below to see how it influences the texture of the drink). The triple-carbonation we do seeks to replicate the "widget" used in Guinness cans (or the nitrogen pressurization used in nitro-brewed coffee), which furthers the silky texture of the beverage.

BREAKFAST STOUT BATCH

- 10g steel cut oats
- 3.5g cinnamon sticks, coarsely crushed
- 30g chocolate malt
- 5g black barley
- 1000g water
- 20g raisins
- 10g cacao nibs
- 1g East Kent Golding hop pellets
- 70g lactose
- 30g powdered dark malt extract
- 15g dark brown sugar

In a medium saucepan, toast the oats over medium heat until fragrant. Add the cinnamon and continue toasting until fragrant. Add the chocolate malt and barley and continue toasting a minute more. Add the water, raisins, and cacao nibs, stirring to combine. Bring the mixture to a boil. Lower heat, cover, and simmer for 20 minutes. Remove from heat, add hops, cover, and allow to steep for 30 more minutes.

Strain the mixture through a fine mesh strainer, discarding solids. Measure 550g of the liquid into a clean bowl. Add the lactose, malt extract, and brown sugar, whisking to dissolve. Allow the mixture to cool, then transfer to the refrigerator to chill completely before carbonating.

Transfer the mixture to a carbonation device. Charge the device with one N_2O cartridge, shaking to dissolve gas. Allow the mixture to settle for 1 minute. Repeat with one more N_2O canister. Finally, charge with one CO_2 cartridge. Reserve in the refrigerator until ready to serve.

TO PORTION AND SERVE

Gently pour 5oz (150ml) of the chilled carbonated batch into a medium serving glass. Serve.

OLIVE OIL

This drink celebrates the bright, grassy flavors often featured in freshly-pressed extra virgin olive oil. The striking, milky appearance – achieved by emulsifying olive oil into the mixture – belies the clean mouthfeel and crisp flavors of the drink. We originally designed it to pair with rich *cacio e pepe* – pasta with Pecorina Romano and black pepper – but it also works well with grilled fish or bacon-wrapped scallops.

HERB STOCK

- 600g water
- 14g fresh lemongrass, crushed and roughly chopped
- 9g fresh tarragon leaves and stems
- 9g fresh mint leaves and stems
- 5g fresh meyer lemon peels, removed with a peeler
- 4.5g fresh thyme leaves and stems
- 4.5g vegetable glycerin

If you have sous vide equipment:
Combine all ingredients in a vacuum bag and seal. Cook en sous vide at 75°C (170°F) for 30 minutes. Meanwhile, prepare an ice bath. When the herb mixture is done, transfer the bag to the ice bath to chill it completely.

If you don't have sous vide equipment:
Fill a small pot with an inch or so of water, and bring it to a simmer over medium-high heat. Combine all ingredients in a metal non-reactive mixing bowl, and cover tightly with plastic wrap or tinfoil. Set this bowl over the simmering pot of water and heat for 30 minutes. Meanwhile, prepare an ice bath. When the herb mixture is done, transfer the covered bowl to the ice bath to chill it completely.

Strain the mixture through a fine mesh strainer, discarding the solids. Transfer the liquid to an airtight container and reserve.

STABILIZER POWDER

- 9g gum arabic
- 1g xanthan gum

In a small bowl, combine the gum arabic and xanthan gum, stirring to mix thoroughly. Reserve the powder in an airtight container.

OLIVE OIL BATCH

- 522g herb stock
- 150g verjus blanc
- 44g sugar
- 1g kosher salt
- 1g stabilizer powder
- 22g extra virgin olive oil

Combine all ingredients except the olive oil in a blender, and blend on high speed for 30 seconds. With blender running at low speed, slowly drizzle in the olive oil, continuing to blend to allow the oil to emulsify. Transfer the mixture to an airtight container. Reserve in the refrigerator to chill thoroughly.

TO PORTION AND SERVE

Pour 3oz (90ml) of the chilled batch into a medium serving glass. Serve.

Note: it is normal for this drink to separate over time. Shake the mixture aggressively or blend it for several seconds to re-emulsify the oil.

CHICHA MORADA

Chicha morada is a bright, refreshing Peruvian drink made from purple corn, pineapple, and baking spices like clove and cinnamon. Here we're lightly adapting these flavors into the form of a cocktail. In addition to being visually-stunning and delicious, purple corn has the added benefit of being rich in antioxidants.

TOASTED COCONUT

- 50g unsweetened coconut flakes

Preheat an oven to 350°F (175°C). Spread the coconut flakes onto a cookie sheet or sheet tray. Toast the flakes in the oven, stirring occasionally, for about 15 minutes, or until brown and very fragrant. Let cool completely. Reserve.

CHICHA MORADA BASE BATCH

- 600g water
- 200g purple corn
- 200g fresh pineapple with skin on, roughly chopped
- 95g fresh limes, quartered
- 30g cinnamon sticks, coarsely crushed
- 25g toasted coconut
- 2g whole cloves

Combine all ingredients in a medium saucepan, cover, and bring to a boil. Remove from heat and allow to steep for 30 minutes. Strain the mixture through a fine mesh strainer, discarding solids. Allow to cool completely. Transfer the liquid to an airtight container. Reserve in the refrigerator.

TO ASSEMBLE AND SERVE

- 1½oz (45ml) chicha morada base
- ¾oz (22.5ml) fresh pineapple juice, extracted with a juicer
- ¾oz (22.5ml) fresh lime juice
- ½oz (15ml) simple syrup *(page 22)*
- 1 egg white
- 1 dash aromatic bitters *(page 35)*

Combine all ingredients in a cocktail shaker. Dry shake until frothy. Add ice and shake again until chilled and diluted, then double-strain into a medium glass. Garnish with 5 additional drops of aromatic bitters. Serve.

$5 SHAKE

One of the courses on our *Hollywood* menu at Next in 2017 – inspired by an infamous scene in Quentin Tarantino's *Pulp Fiction* – involved a playful take on a burger with fries. The pairing we developed for this was obvious: we wanted to make a really good milkshake.

To do this, we make a classic custard to serve as our ice cream base. This involves gently warming egg yolks with cream, which – if done properly – yields a thick mixture that takes on a lovely soft texture when frozen. We flavor our custard opulently with saffron and tonka beans, the latter of which offers an enigmatically complex note reminiscent of vanilla, cinnamon, and honey (if you cannot source tonka beans, substituting a whole vanilla bean and a sprinkle of cinnamon works reasonably well).

Our ice cream base is combined with a milk infused with sassafras, the main flavor found in root beer. The shake is topped with hand-whipped cream and, of course, a cherry. It's the perfect drink to get you ready to win a dance contest.

TONKA SAFFRON ICE CREAM BASE

3 egg yolks
75g sugar
1g kosher salt
5g tonka beans, coarsely crushed
300g heavy cream
100g buttermilk
1g saffron threads

Fill a large bowl with ice, and set a smaller bowl inside it.

Combine the egg yolks, sugar, and salt in a medium bowl, whisking to mix thoroughly. Set aside.

Toast the tonka beans in a medium saucepan over medium heat until fragrant. Add the heavy cream, buttermilk, and saffron, stirring to combine thoroughly. Heat the mixture to 120°F (50°C), stirring constantly to prevent milk from scalding. Remove the saucepan from the heat. Working in small increments, slowly whisk the heated cream into the egg mixture.

Fill a small pot with an inch or so of water, and bring it to a simmer over medium-high heat. Place the bowl containing the egg and cream mixture over the simmering water and begin whisking (this helps prevent the eggs from curdling). Heat the mixture to around 155°F (70°C) – or until it's uncomfortable to dip your finger into the mixture for more than a second or so – whisking constantly as it warms.

Remove from heat and strain the mixture through a fine mesh strainer into the bowl set over ice. Allow the mixture to cool completely. Reserve in the refrigerator to chill thoroughly.

$5 Shake, continued

SASSAFRAS MILK

- 200g milk
- 20g sassafras or sarsaparilla root, coarsely crushed
- 16g sugar
- 1g kosher salt

Combine the milk and sassafras root in a medium saucepan and bring to a simmer over medium heat, stirring constantly. Remove from heat, cover, and allow to steep for 20 minutes. Strain the mixture through a fine mesh strainer, discarding solids. Add the sugar and salt, whisking to dissolve completely. Reserve in the refrigerator.

$5 Shake, continued

WHIPPED CREAM

200 g heavy cream
25 g powdered sugar
0.5 g kosher salt

If you have a cream whipper canister:
Combine all ingredients in a small bowl, whisking briefly to dissolve sugar and salt. Transfer to the canister of a cream whipper, and charge with two N_2O cartridges, shaking vigorously after each charge. Transfer the canister to the refrigerator to chill thoroughly.

If you have a stand mixer:
Combine all ingredients in the bowl of a stand mixer fitted with the whisk attachment. Whisk at high speed until stiff peaks form. Transfer the mixture to a covered container or a pastry bag fitted with a decorative tip and reserve in the refrigerator.

If you do not have a stand mixer:
Combine all ingredients in a large mixing bowl. Whisk until stiff peaks form. Transfer the mixture to a covered container or a pastry bag fitted with a decorative tip and reserve in the refrigerator.

TO ASSEMBLE AND SERVE

450 g tonka saffron ice cream base
100 g sassafras milk
1 tonka bean
1 Luxardo cherry

To freeze and serve using liquid nitrogen:
In a small bowl, whisk together the ice cream base and sassafras milk while slowly adding liquid nitrogen until the mixture is thick and slushy. Transfer the mixture to a tall serving glass. Pipe or spoon whipped cream onto the shake. Garnish with a grating of tonka bean and top with a cherry.

To freeze and serve using an ice cream maker:
Combine the ice cream base and sassafras milk in the bowl of an ice cream churn. Churn according to the manufacturer's instructions until the mixture is thick and slushy. Transfer the mixture to a tall serving glass. Pipe or spoon whipped cream onto the shake. Garnish with a grating of tonka bean and top with a cherry.

To freeze and serve using a conventional freezer:
Combine the ice cream base and sassafras milk in a shallow container and transfer to the freezer. Using a fork, scrape the mixture every 20–30 minutes, breaking up any ice crystals that form. Repeat until the mixture becomes thick and slushy. Transfer the mixture to a tall serving glass. Pipe or spoon whipped cream onto the shake. Garnish with a grating of tonka bean and top with a cherry.

TZATZIKI

Greek-style *tzatziki* is a yogurt-based cucumber dip often served as an appetizer or a side dish accompanying meat. While traditional *tzatziki* includes savory ingredients like garlic and salt, we omit these and choose instead to sweeten the drink with a bit of honey, which keeps it light and refreshing while preserving the original flavor profile. Tasty on its own, this one also pairs very well with grilled foods.

MINT TEA

- 350 g water
- 10 g Rare Tea Cellar Mint Meritage tea

In a medium saucepan, bring the water to a boil. Remove from heat. Measure 300 g of the hot water into a separate bowl, and add tea. Cover and let steep for 8 minutes. Strain the tea through a fine mesh strainer, discarding solids. Reserve in the refrigerator.

CUCUMBER MINT STOCK

- 600 g water
- 125 g English cucumber, peeled and coarsely chopped
- 1 g citric acid
- 200 g reserved mint tea

Combine the water and English cucumber in a blender. Blend on high speed for 30 seconds. Strain the mixture through a fine mesh strainer into a clean bowl, discarding solids. Add the citric acid, cover, and allow the mixture to sit in the refrigerator overnight; fine solids will settle to the bottom of the bowl. Gently pour the clarified liquid from the bowl into a clean container, taking care not to disturb the sediment and leaving as much of it behind as possible. Add the reserved mint tea, stirring to combine. Reserve in the refrigerator to chill thoroughly.

CARDAMOM LIME STOCK

- 3 g whole green cardamom pods, coarsely crushed
- 270 g water
- 1 g Rare Tea Cellar Black Limes

In a medium saucepan, toast the cardamom over medium heat until fragrant. Add the remaining ingredients and bring to a boil. Lower heat, cover, and simmer for 5 minutes. Remove from heat and allow to steep for 20 minutes. Strain the mixture through a fine mesh strainer, discarding solids. Reserve in the refrigerator.

CARDAMOM YOGURT

- 190 g cardamom lime stock
- 95 g nonfat Greek yogurt
- 80 g honey
- 28 g sugar
- 2 g lactic acid
- 1 g kosher salt

Combine all ingredients in a mixing bowl, whisking to dissolve sugar, acid, and salt. Transfer to an airtight container and reserve in the refrigerator to chill thoroughly.

CUCUMBER RIBBONS

- 1 English cucumber

Remove the peel from the cucumber using a vegetable peeler, then use the peeler to slice the cucumber into long, thin ribbons. Trim the ends of the ribbons with a sharp knife to neaten them. Stack the ribbons and reserve them in the refrigerator between two damp paper towels.

TO ASSEMBLE AND SERVE

- 1 cucumber ribbon
- 3 oz (90 ml) cucumber mint stock
- 2 oz (60 ml) cardamom yogurt
- 1 mint sprig

Place a cucumber ribbon into a medium serving glass, pressing it against the side of the glass to help hold it in place. Fill the glass three-quarters full of ice. Add the cucumber mint stock, then cardamom yogurt. Garnish with a fresh sprig of mint. Serve with a straw, using the straw to stir the ingredients together.

HONG KONG MILK TEA

Hong Kong-style milk tea is a classic beverage consisting of black tea, evaporated milk, and sugar. The exact blend of teas used varies widely, with most being closely guarded secrets of the tea vendors that sell the drink. Our recipe combines a traditional English Breakfast blend with rose and chicory for added depth and complexity.

CHICORY TEA

- 150 g water
- 6 g Rare Tea Cellar Fresh Roasted French Chicory

In a medium saucepan, bring the water to a boil. Remove from heat. Measure 100 g of the hot water into a separate bowl and add chicory. Cover and let steep for 8 minutes. Strain the mixture through a fine mesh strainer, discarding solids. Transfer the liquid to an airtight container and reserve.

ROSE TEA BLEND

- 600 g water
- 11 g Rare Tea Cellar Rose Noir tea
- 11 g Rare Tea Cellar Regal English Breakfast tea
- 11 g rose hips

In a medium saucepan, bring the water to a boil. Remove from heat. Measure 550 g of the hot water into a separate bowl, then add teas and rose hips, stirring to combine. Cover and let steep for 8 minutes. Strain the tea through a fine mesh strainer, discarding solids. Transfer the liquid to an airtight container and reserve.

HONG KONG MILK TEA BATCH

- 470 g rose tea blend
- 155 g evaporated milk
- 85 g chicory tea
- 55 g sugar

Combine all ingredients in a mixing bowl, whisking to dissolve sugar. Transfer to an airtight container and reserve in the refrigerator to chill thoroughly.

TO PORTION AND SERVE

Pour 3 oz (90 ml) of the chilled batch into a medium serving glass. Serve.

LEMON HORCHATA

While the *horchata* found in Mexican restaurants throughout the U.S. is typically made with rice (and is sweetened with sugar and cinnamon), the drink originated in Spain, where it was originally prepared from sweetened, almond-like tiger nuts. Here we build on these origins, adding flavor complexity with the use of a lemon syrup that we cook with mace and peppercorns.

LEMON OLEO SACCHARUM

- 3 lemons
- 100 g sugar
- 100 g water

Peel the lemons with a vegetable peeler, taking care to remove as little pith as possible. Reserve the fruit for another use.

In a medium bowl, combine the lemon peels and sugar. Muddle the mixture with a spoon or a cocktail muddler. Cover and allow to sit for at least 4 hours or overnight, muddling and stirring periodically.

In a small saucepan, bring the water to a simmer. Pour the hot water over the lemon peels, stirring to dissolve the sugar. Strain the mixture through a fine mesh strainer, discarding solids. Transfer to an airtight container and reserve in the refrigerator.

LEMON PEPPER SYRUP

- 110 g lemon oleo saccharum
- 12 g Marcona almonds
- 6 g whole white peppercorns
- 1 g blade mace

Combine all ingredients in a small saucepan and bring to a boil over medium heat. Remove from heat and transfer to a blender. Pulse once or twice to break up the almonds and blade mace, then cover and set aside until completely cooled. Strain the mixture through a fine mesh strainer, discarding solids. Transfer to an airtight container and reserve in the refrigerator.

Lemon Horchata, continued

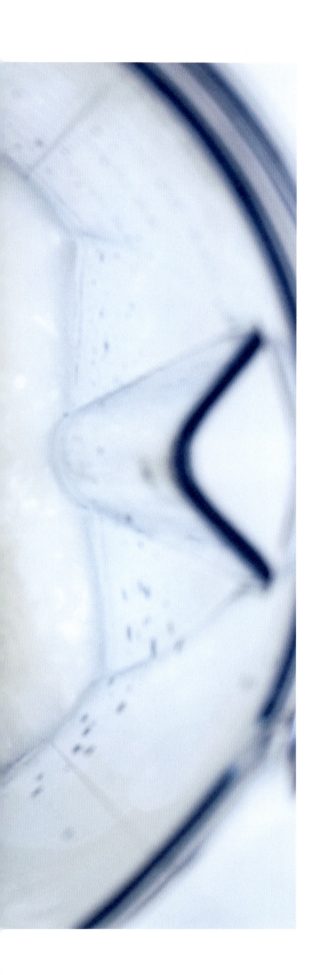

MARCONA RICE MILK

| 125 g Marcona almonds
| 145 g jasmine rice
| 1400 g water

Place the almonds in a small bowl and add enough water to cover. Stir the almonds thoroughly, then strain and rinse to remove any surface salt.

In a medium bowl, combine the almonds, rice, and water. Allow to soak for 24 hours in the refrigerator. Transfer the mixture to a blender and blend on high speed for 30 seconds. Strain through a fine mesh strainer into a clean bowl, discarding solids. Allow the mixture to sit for 45 minutes; the starches will settle to the bottom of the bowl. Gently pour the liquid from the bowl into a clean container, taking care not to disturb settled starches and leaving as much of them behind as possible. Transfer the rice milk to an airtight container. Reserve in the refrigerator.

LEMON HORCHATA BATCH

| 720 g Marcona rice milk
| 70 g lemon pepper syrup
| 50 g sugar
| 2 g kosher salt

Combine all ingredients in a mixing bowl, whisking to dissolve salt. Transfer to an airtight container and reserve in the refrigerator to chill thoroughly.

TO PORTION AND SERVE

Fill a medium serving glass three-quarters full of ice cubes. Pour the chilled horchata over the ice. Serve.

PEANUT BUTTER & BANANA SANDWICH

RICE MILK

| 1100g hot water
| 175g jasmine rice

In a medium bowl, combine the water and rice. Allow to soak for at least 2 hours. Transfer the mixture to a blender and blend on high speed for 30 seconds. Strain through a fine mesh strainer into a clean bowl, discarding solids. Allow the mixture to sit for 45 minutes; the starches will settle to the bottom of the bowl. Gently pour the liquid from the bowl into a clean container, taking care not to disturb settled starches and leaving as much of them behind as possible. Transfer the rice milk to an airtight container. Reserve.

PEANUT BUTTER & BANANA SANDWICH BATCH

| 575g rice milk
| 155g water
| 150g sugar
| 125g passionfruit purée
| 50g Huilerie Beaujolaise Virgin Grilled Peanut Oil
| 35g bananas
| 1g kosher salt
| 1g xanthan gum

Combine all ingredients in a blender, and blend on high speed for 1 minute. Transfer to an airtight container and reserve in the refrigerator to chill thoroughly.

TO PORTION AND SERVE

Pour 3oz (90ml) of the chilled batch into a medium serving glass. Serve.

LECHE DE TIGRE

Ceviche is a Peruvian seafood preparation in which raw fish is cured in a mixture of citrus juices, chili, and a variety of seasonings including onion, salt, and garlic. Oftentimes, a small glass of this marinade is served alongside the dish. This spicy, full-flavored beverage is referred to as *leche de tigre,* or "tiger's milk".

JALAPEÑO TEA

- 850 g water
- 32 g Rare Tea Cellar Ancient Tea Tree Flowers
- 20 g jalapeños, thinly sliced (seeds included)

In a medium saucepan, bring the water to a boil. Remove from heat. Measure 800 g of the hot water into a separate bowl, and add the tea and jalapeños. Cover and let steep for 7 minutes. Strain the mixture through a fine mesh strainer, discarding solids. Transfer the liquid to an airtight container and reserve in the refrigerator to chill thoroughly.

ONION GARLIC PURÉE

- 50 g green onions
- 50 g elephant garlic

Fill a medium saucepan with water and bring to a boil over high heat. Meanwhile, fill a large bowl with ice water. Slice the green onions and elephant garlic bulbs thinly using a sharp knife or mandoline. Blanch the onions and garlic in boiling water for 1 minute, then immediately transfer to the ice water. Drain the onions and garlic, squeezing out excess water.

Place a blender pitcher on a scale, and add the blanched onions and garlic. Add an equal weight of water, and blend on high speed for 1 minute, or until perfectly smooth. Strain the mixture through a fine mesh strainer, discarding any solids. Reserve.

Leche de Tigre, continued

PRICKLY PEAR BASE BATCH

720 g prickly pear purée
105 g fresh ginger juice, extracted with a juicer
100 g onion garlic purée
95 g sugar
9 g citric acid
2 g kosher salt

Combine all ingredients in a mixing bowl, whisking to dissolve sugar, acid, and salt. Transfer to an airtight container and reserve in the refrigerator to chill thoroughly.

TO ASSEMBLE AND SERVE

100 g prickly pear base
70 g jalapeño tea

In a medium serving glass, stir together the prickly pear base with the jalapeño tea. Serve.

Leche de Tigre, continued

SOFT CIDER

The process of fermenting apples to produce "hard" cider replaces the typical sweetness of apple juice with a host of funky, yeastlike flavors. Fascinated by this, we wanted to see if we could replicate these interesting flavors in a non-alcoholic beverage.

YEASTED HERB STOCK

- 1.5g Red Star Premier Blanc Champagne yeast
- 1g anise seeds, coarsely crushed
- 1g juniper berries, coarsely crushed
- 200g water
- 0.5g dried Herbes des Provence

In a medium saucepan, toast the yeast, anise seeds, and juniper over medium heat until fragrant. Add the remaining ingredients and bring to a boil. Remove from heat, cover, and allow to steep for 30 minutes. Strain the mixture through a fine mesh strainer, discarding solids. Transfer to an airtight container and reserve in the refrigerator to chill thoroughly.

SOFT CIDER BATCH

- 560g fresh unfiltered apple cider
- 115g yeasted herb stock
- 80g water
- 15g sugar
- 7.5g low-sodium tamari
- 4g fish sauce
- 1.5g malic acid

Combine all ingredients in a mixing bowl, whisking to dissolve sugar. Transfer to a carbonation device, and chill thoroughly in the refrigerator or in an ice bath. Carbonate according to manufacturer's instructions. Reserve in the refrigerator.

TO PORTION AND SERVE

Gently pour 5oz (150ml) of the chilled batch into a medium serving glass. Serve.

LIMONCELLO

Traditional limoncello is a sweet Italian liqueur made by soaking lemon peels in a distilled spirit such as grappa or vodka. Oil from the peels is absorbed into the alcohol, yielding a bright, aromatic liquid tasting richly of lemon.

We start our limoncello by first making a citrus syrup; in this case, we use a Buddha's hand citron, which has a bright, floral quality, but the peel and pith of lemon is an easy substitute. We next make a "pudding" by cooking condensed milk with agar agar, a technique that stabilizes the milk and prevents it from curdling and separating when we later mix it with lemon juice. Combining these yields a creamy, sweet "liqueur" that works well with desserts or as an after-dinner *digestivo*.

BUDDHA'S HAND JAM

- 380g water
- 340g sugar
- 125g fresh pineapple, peel removed, diced
- 90g fresh Buddha's hand citron, diced

Combine all ingredients in a medium saucepan. Bring the mixture to boil over high heat, then lower to a simmer. Cook the mixture until it measures 219°F (104°C) on a candy thermometer. Remove from heat and strain the mixture through a fine mesh strainer, discarding solids (or reserving them for another use). Allow the strained liquid to cool completely. Reserve in an airtight container.

CONDENSED MILK PUDDING

- 200g sweetened condensed milk
- 100g whole milk
- 1g agar agar

Fill a large bowl with ice water. Combine all ingredients in a medium saucepan. Bring the mixture to a boil, whisking constantly. Boil for 1 minute. Remove from heat, and place the pan in ice water until the pudding completely cools and sets. Transfer to a blender and blend on high speed until very smooth. Strain the mixture through a fine mesh strainer. Reserve in an airtight container in the refrigerator.

LIMONCELLO BATCH

- 460g water
- 250g condensed milk pudding
- 250g Buddha's hand jam
- 90g sugar
- 70g fresh lemon juice

Combine all ingredients in a blender, and blend on high speed for 30 seconds. Strain the mixture through a fine mesh strainer, discarding solids. Transfer to an airtight container and reserve in the refrigerator to chill thoroughly.

TO PORTION AND SERVE

- 1 lemon peel, removed with a channel knife

Pour 2oz (60ml) of the chilled batch into a small serving glass. Express the lemon peel over the glass, then garnish the glass with the peel. Serve.

INDEX

INDEX

A

Absinthe, 55
Absinthe Syrup, 55
    in Death in the Afternoon, 56
agar agar, in Condensed Milk Pudding for Limoncello, 235
agave syrup
    in Mezcal, 32
    in Pechuga, 141
    in Tequila, 30
ajowan seeds, in Fruitcake Ice for Sparkling Plum Sour, 79
allspice
    in Aromatic Bitters, 35
    in Falernum for Sparkling Plum Sour, 80
    in Jamaican Rum, 37
    in Peach Vinegar for Peach Shrub, 197
    in Return of the Mac, 91
    in Spiced Barley Stock for Cereal Killer, 69
    in Spiced Pear Syrup for Americano, 131
    in Sun Dried, 187
almonds, Marcona
    in Lemon Pepper Syrup for Lemon Horchata for Lemon Horchata, 223
    Marcona Rice Milk for Lemon Horchata, 225
aloe leaf powder, in Fernet, 41
aloe vera juice
    in Golden Glow, 101
    in What Would Honeydew, 73
Amaro, 38
    in Black Manhattan, 59
    See also Bitter Amaro
Amaro & Coke, 60
Americano, 130–1
American Whiskey, 29
    in Black Manhattan, 59
    in Whiskey Sour, 58
angelica root
    in Amaro, 38
    in Bitter Amaro, 36
    in Bitter Apéritif for Americano, 131
    in Bitter Liqueur, 42
    in Clarified Lime Cucumber for What Would Honeydew, 71
    in Gin, 28
Angostura Aromatic Bitters, See Aromatic Bitters
anise seeds
    in Amaro, 38
    in Yeasted Herb Stock for Soft Cider, 233
apple cider
    in Return of the Mac, 91
    in Soft Cider, 233
apple juice, in Return of the Mac, 91
apples
    McIntosh Apple Slices, 90, 91
    Return of the Mac, 88–91
apricots
    in Mezcal, 32
    in Tequila, 30
Aromatic Bitters, 35
    in Chicha Morada, 213
    in Sparkling Plum Sour, 81
artichokes, in Bitter Amaro, 36
Averna Amaro, See Amaro

B

backbar recipes, 25–42
banana chips, in Lovely Bunch, 155
bananas
    in American Whiskey, 29
    Banana Chai, 176–9
    Banana Milk Punch for Banana Chai, 178
    in Jamaican Rum, 37
    Lovely Bunch, 155
    Peanut Butter & Banana Sandwich, 226–7
    Roasted Banana for Banana Chai, 177
    Roasted Banana Peel for Lovely Bunch, 155
barley
    in American Whiskey, 29
    Barley Stock for Korean Spiced Margarita, 83
    in Breakfast Stout, 209
    Spiced Barley Stock for Cereal Killer, 69
barley, malted
    in American Whiskey, 29
    in Spiced Barley Stock for Cereal Killer, 69
basil
    in Bitter Amaro, 36
    in Grapefruit Jicama Champagne, 171
    in Green Herb Vinegar for Green Herb Shrub, 203
    in Herbal Liqueur, 40
basil, Thai, in Green Herb Vinegar for Green Herb Shrub, 203
bay leaves
    in Mezcal, 32
    in Strawberry Tomato, 192
    in Tequila, 30
BBQ, 92–3
BBQ Stock for BBQ, 93
beer
    Breakfast Stout, 208–9
    IPA, 158–61
beet juice, in Umami Bomb, 205
bell peppers
    in Golden Glow, 101
    in Paprika Milk Punch, 87
    in Serrano Ice for Celery Serrano, 122
bergamot purée, in Truffled Cherry, 173
Bijou, 61
Bitter Amaro, 36
    in Amaro & Coke, 60
Bitter Apéritif, 131
Bitter Liqueur, 42
    in Jungle Bird, 51
    in Negroni, 62
Bitter Orange Tincture for Peach Shrub, 197
bitters
    alcohol content of, 69
    chocolate bitters in Instant Oatmeal, 125
    See also Aromatic Bitters; black walnut bitters; Orange Bitters
blackberries
    Blackberry Pomegranate Syrup for Bramblin' Man, 143
    Blackberry Syrup for Cereal Killer, 69
    in Mole, 165
Black Garlic Purée for Umami Bomb, 205
black lime, in Cardamom Lime Stock for Tzatziki, 219
Black Manhattan, 59
black peppercorns, See peppercorns, black
Black Pepper Stock for Golden Glow, 101
Black Rice Stock for Self-Carbonating Cinnamon Passionfruit Fizz, 147
Blackstrap Rum, 33
    in Jungle Bird, 51
black walnut bitters
    in Americano, 131
    in Cereal Killer, 69
    in Instant Oatmeal, 125
    in Salted Caramel Cherry, 151
    in Smoked Strawberry Old Fashioned, 117
blenders, about, 18
blood oranges
    Curry Blood Oranges for Lovely Bunch, 153, 155
    in Room for Dessert?, 183
blueberry juice
    in Blueberry Pancakes, 201
    in Spiced Blueberry Shrub, 189
Blueberry Pancakes, 198–201

INDEX *continued*

Blueberry Shrub, Spiced, 189
Bramblin' Man, 142–3
Breakfast Stout, 208–9
brine, in Salad, 75
Brown Butter Stock for Blueberry Pancakes, 199, 201
Bruto Americano, See Bitter Apéritif
Bubblegum, 94–7
Bubblegum Stock for Bubblegum, 96, 97
Buddha's Hand Jam for Limoncello, 235
buttermilk, in Tonka Saffron Ice Cream for $5 Shake, 215
Butternut Squash Stock for Pretzel, 139
Butter Stock, Brown, for Blueberry Pancakes, 199, 201

C

cacao nibs
    in Breakfast Stout, 209
    in Butternut Squash Stock for Pretzel, 139
    in Mole, 165
    in Spanish Rum, 33
Campari, See Bitter Liqueur
cane syrup
    in Fernet, 41
    in Umami Bomb, 205
cane vinegar, See vinegar, cane
Caramel Pu-erh Tea for Salted Caramel Cherry, 151
caraway seeds, in Orange Bitters, 34
carbonation devices, 18
cardamom, black
    in Fruitcake Ice for Sparkling Plum Sour, 79
    in Jamaican Rum, 37
    in Mezcal, 32
cardamom, green
    in Aromatic Bitters, 35
    Cardamom Lime Stock for Tzatziki, 219
    Cardamom Port, 180–1
    Cardamom Yogurt for Tzatziki, 219
    Chile Cardamom Stock, 181
    in Fernet, 41
    in Fruitcake Ice for Sparkling Plum Sour, 79
    in Gin, 28
    in Green Herb Vinegar for Green Herb Shrub, 203
    in Herbal Liqueur, 40
    in Orange Bitters, 34
    in Return of the Mac, 91
    in Sweet Vermouth, 39
    in Tzatziki, 219
cardamom, red, in Cardamom Port, 181
carob syrup, in Cereal Killer, 69
cashews, in Falernum for Sparkling Plum Sour, 80
celery
    Celery Serrano, 120–3
    Celery Stock for Celery Serrano, 121, 122
    in Down to Earth, 85
centrifugal juicers, 19
Cereal Killer, 68–9
chai tea
    Banana Chai, 177, 178
    in Lovely Bunch, 155
chamomile
    in Bitter Apéritif for Americano, 131
    in Sweet Vermouth, 39
champagnes
    Grapefruit Jicama Champagne, 170–1
    Lychee Champagne, 194–5
    Rose Champagne, 184–5
channel knife, about, 19
Charred Strawberries for BBQ, 93
Chartreuse, See Herbal Liqueur
cherries, dried, in Sweet Vermouth, 39

cherry juice, tart
    in Pretzel, 139
    in Salted Caramel Cherry, 151
    in Truffled Cherry, 173
Chicha Morada, 212–13
Chicken Broth for Pechuga, 141
chicory
    in Amaro, 38
    Chicory Tea for Hong Kong Milk Tea, 221
    Coffee Chicory Stock for Room for Dessert?, 183
Chile Cardamom Stock for Cardamom Port, 181
chiles, ancho
    in Lovely Bunch, 155
    in Mole, 165
chiles, guajillo
    in Chile Cardamom Stock for Cardamom Port, 181
    in Mole, 165
chiles, jalapeño
    Jalapeño Tea for Leche de Tigre, 229, 230
    in Mezcal, 32
    in Tequila, 30
chiles, poblano, in Herbal Liqueur, 40
chilies, Fresno, in Hot Sauce Ice for Margarita, 53
chilies, serrano
    Celery Serrano, 120–3
    Serrano Ice, 122
chilies, Thai, in Thai Stock for Thai Fighter, 115
Chili Powder Mix for Korean Spiced Margarita, 83
chipotles, in BBQ Stock for BBQ, 93
chitosan
    in Clarified Lime Cucumber for What Would Honeydew, 71
    in Rose Champagne, 185
chocolate, white
    Sparkling White Chocolate & Guava Consommé, 108–9
    White Chocolate Syrup for Room for Dessert?, 183
    See also cacao nibs; cocoa powder
chocolate bitters, in Instant Oatmeal, 125
chocolate malt, in Breakfast Stout, 209
Chrysanthemum Tea for Mum's The Word, 111, 112
cider
    in Return of the Mac, 91
    Soft Cider, 232–3
cider-spiced tea, in Return of the Mac, 91
cinchona bark
    in Bitter Amaro, 36
    in Fernet, 41
    in Orange Bitters, 34
    in Sweet Vermouth, 39
cinnamon sticks
    in Bitter Liqueur, 42
    in Breakfast Stout, 209
    in Chicha Morada, 213
    Cinnamon Stock for Passionfruit Cocktail, 147
    in Falernum for Sparkling Plum Sour, 80
    in Fruitcake Ice for Sparkling Plum Sour, 79
    in Herbal Liqueur, 40
    in Mole, 165
    in Orange Liqueur, 31
    in Return of the Mac, 91
    in Spiced Barley Stock for Cereal Killer, 69
    in Spiced Pear Syrup for Americano, 131
    in Sun Dried, 187
    in Tamarind Coriander Stock for Shake Your Tamarind, 77
    in 3-Spiced Vinegar for Spiced Blueberry Shrub, 189
Citra hops, in Hop Stock for IPA, 159
Citrus Oleo Saccharum for Bubblegum, 95, 97
citrus peels, expressing, 21
clarification, 17, 117, 159, 160
Clarified Lime Cucumber for What Would Honeydew, 71, 73
Clarified Passionfruit Mango Stock for IPA, 160
Clarified Rhubarb Juice for Rhubarb, Thyme, Juniper, 163

INDEX *continued*

clarity, 17, 21
classic cocktails, 45–62
cloves
    in Amaro, 38
    in Aromatic Bitters, 35
    in Bitter Liqueur, 42
    in Chicha Morada, 213
    in Falernum for Sparkling Plum Sour, 80
    in Fruitcake Ice for Sparkling Plum Sour, 79
    in Herbal Liqueur, 40
    in Mole, 165
    in Orange Bitters, 34
    in Orange Liqueur, 31
    in Sweet Vermouth, 39
Coca-Cola
    in Amaro & Coke, 60
    in Bitter Amaro, 36
cocktail shakers, about, 18
cocktail strainers, about, 19, 21
cocoa powder, in Banana Milk Punch for Banana Chai, 178
coconut, in Toasted Coconut for Chicha Morada, 213
coconut aminos, in BBQ, 93
coconut water, in Golden Glow, 101
Coffee Chicory Stock for Room for Dessert?, 183
Cointreau, See Orange Liqueur
Condensed Milk Pudding for Limoncello, 235
coriander seeds
    in Amaro, 38
    Coriander Stock for Pechuga, 141
    in Gin, 28
    in Green Herb Vinegar for Green Herb Shrub, 203
    in Herbal Liqueur, 40
    in Mezcal, 32
    in Sweet Vermouth, 39
    Tamarind Coriander Stock for Shake Your Tamarind, 77
    in Thai Stock for Thai Fighter, 115
corn
    in Chicha Morada, 213
    Sweet Corn, 133
cream, heavy
    in Tonka Saffron Ice Cream for $5 Shake, 215
    Whipped Cream for $5 Shake, 217
Crodino, in Watermelon Ginger Tonic, 128
cucumber
    Clarified Lime Cucumber in What Would Honeydew, 71, 73
    Cucumber Mint Stock for Tzatziki, 219
    in Tzatziki, 219
cumin seeds
    in BBQ Stock for BBQ, 93
    in Spice Mix for Paprika Milk Punch, 87
Curry Blood Oranges for Lovely Bunch, 153, 155
curry powder
    in Curry Blood Oranges for Lovely Bunch, 153
    in Sweet Corn, 133
Cynar, See Bitter Amaro

D

Daiquiri, 50
dates, in Fruitcake Ice for Sparkling Plum Sour, 79
Death in the Afternoon, 56
Demerara Syrup, 22
dilution, 15, 16
double straining, 21
Down to Earth, 84–5
Dr. Pepper, in Sun Dried, 187
dry shaking, 21

E

eggs
    in Green Papaya Salad, 145
    in Sparkling White Chocolate & Guava Consommé, 109
    in Tonka Saffron Ice Cream for $5 Shake, 215
    in Whiskey Sour, 58
English Breakfast tea, in Hong Kong Milk Tea, 221
equipment basics, 18–19
expressing citrus peels, 21

F

Falernum for Sparkling Plum Sour, 80, 81
fennel oil, in Absinthe Syrup, 55
fennel pollen, in Herbal Liqueur, 40
fennel seeds
    in Amaro, 38
    in Gin, 28
    in Herbal Liqueur, 40
fenugreek seeds
    in American Whiskey, 29
    in Fruitcake Ice for Sparkling Plum Sour, 79
    in Herbal Liqueur, 40
    in Sweet Corn, 133
fermentation, 20
Fernet, 41
    in Amaro & Coke, 60
Fig Purée for Sun Dried, 187
figs, dried
    in American Whiskey, 29
    in Bitter Apéritif for Americano, 131
    Fig Purée for Sun Dried, 187
    Fig Stock for Mum's The Word, 111, 112
    Fig Stock for Roasted Sweet Potato, 107
    in Fruitcake Ice for Sparkling Plum Sour, 79
    in Sweet Vermouth, 39
fish sauce
    in Green Papaya Salad, 145
    in Soft Cider, 233
$5 Shake, 214–17
French 75, 57
Fruitcake Ice for Sparkling Plum Sour, 79, 81

G

galangal
    in Fernet, 41
    in Herbal Liqueur, 40
garlic
    Black Garlic Purée for Umami Bomb, 205
    in Marinated Tomatoes for Salad, 75
    Onion Garlic Purée for Leche De Tigre, 229
gelatin clarification, 17, 159, 160
gentian root
    in Amaro, 38
    in Aromatic Bitters, 35
    in Bitter Amaro, 36
    in Bitter Apéritif for Americano, 131
    in Bitter Liqueur, 42
    in Fernet, 41
    in Orange Bitters, 34
    in Sweet Vermouth, 39
Gin, 28
    in Bijou, 61
    in French 75, 57
    in Negroni, 62
ginger
    in Falernum for Sparkling Plum Sour, 80
    in Gin, 28
    Ginger Syrup for Celery Serrano, 121, 122
    Ginger Syrup for Korean Spiced Margarita, 83
    Ginger Syrup for Watermelon Ginger Tonic, 127, 128
    in Herbal Liqueur, 40

INDEX *continued*

in Jamaican Rum, 37
in Mezcal, 32
in Mum's The Word, 112
in Prickly Pear Base for Leche De Tigre, 230
in Serrano Ice for Celery Serrano, 122
in Sweet Vermouth, 39
in Tequila, 30
in Thai Peanut Sauce, 119
in Thai Stock for Thai Fighter, 115
Watermelon Ginger Tonic, 126–9
ginger, powdered, in Aromatic Bitters, 35
glassware, about, 21
glycerin, vegetable
in Absinthe Syrup, 55
in Bitter Apéritif for Americano, 131
in Bitter Orange Tincture for Peach Shrub, 197
in Bubblegum, 97
in Gin, 28
in Grapefruit Turmeric Shrub, 175
in Herbal Liqueur, 40
in Herb Stock for Olive Oil, 211
in Lemongrass Kaffir Stock for Summer Summer, 135
in Orange Bitters, 34
in Spiced Blueberry Shrub, 189
Gochujang Syrup for Korean Spiced Margarita, 83
Golden Glow, 100–1
grapefruit
in Bitter Apéritif for Americano, 131
in Bitter Liqueur, 42
Grapefruit Jicama Champagne, 171
Grapefruit Mimosa, 48
Grapefruit Turmeric Shrub, 174–175
Grapefruit Vinegar for Grapefruit Turmeric Shrub, 175
in Paloma, 49
in Thai Fighter, 115
in Watermelon Ginger Tonic, 129
grape juice, Concord
in Me & You, 157
in Umami Bomb, 205
grape juice, white
in Grapefruit Jicama Champagne, 171
in Watermelon Ginger Tonic, 128
grapes, in Nectarine White Grape Stock for New Millennium, 104
graters, about, 19
Green Herb Shrub, 202–3
Green Herb Vinegar for Green Herb Shrub, 203
green olive brine, in Salad, 75
green onions, in Onion Garlic Purée for Leche De Tigre, 229
Green Papaya Salad, 144–5
guava
Guava Purée, 109
Sparkling White Chocolate & Guava Consommé, 108–9

H

Hawthorne strainers, about, 19, 21
Herbal Liqueur, 40
in Bijou, 61
Herbes des Provence, in Yeasted Herb Stock for Soft Cider, 233
Herb Shrub, Green, 202–3
Herb Stock, Yeasted, 233
Herb Stock for Olive Oil, 211
Herb Vinegar, Green, 203
hibiscus flowers, dried
in Bitter Apéritif for Americano, 131
in Chile Cardamom Stock for Cardamom Port, 181
in Grapefruit Vinegar for Grapefruit Turmeric Shrub, 175
in Return of the Mac, 91
honey
in Cardamom Yogurt for Tzatziki, 219
in Herbal Liqueur, 40
in Me & You, 157

honeydew melon
Mint Honeydew Ice, 73
What Would Honeydew, 70–3
Hong Kong Milk Tea, 220–1
hops
in Breakfast Stout, 209
Hop Stock for IPA, 159, 160
Horchata, Lemon, 222–5
horseradish, in Green Papaya Salad, 145
Hot Sauce Ice for Margarita, 53

I

ice
equipment for, 19
Fruitcake Ice, 79, 81
Hot Sauce Ice, 53
Lavender Watermelon Ice, 135
Mint Honeydew Ice, 73
Serrano Ice, 122
Smoke Ice, 103, 105
tips for chilling drinks, 21
Ice Cream, Tonka Saffron, for $5 Shake, 215, 217
ice wine tea
in Pechuga, 141
in Spiced Blueberry Shrub, 189
Instant Oatmeal, 11, 124–5
IPA, 158–61

J

jalapeño chiles, See chiles, jalapeño
Jalapeño Tea for Leche de Tigre, 229, 230
Jamaican Rum, 37
in Daiquiri, 50
Jasmine Stock for Snap Pea, 149
jicama
in Down to Earth, 85
Grapefruit Jicama Champagne, 171
jiggers, about, 19
juicers, about, 19
Jungle Bird, 51
Juniper, Rhubarb, Thyme, 162–3
juniper berries
in Gin, 28
Juniper Raisin, 98–99
in Yeasted Herb Stock for Soft Cider, 233

K

kaffir lime leaves
Lemongrass Kaffir Stock for Summer Summer, 135, 136
in Thai Stock for Thai Fighter, 115
kalamansi purée, in Shake Your Tamarind, 77
kieselsol
in Clarified Lime Cucumber for What Would Honeydew, 71
in Rose Champagne, 185
Korean Spiced Margarita, 82–3

L

lactose, in Breakfast Stout, 209
lapsang souchong tea
in Mezcal, 32
in Smoked Strawberry Old Fashioned, 117
in Smoke Ice for New Millennium, 103
Lavender Watermelon Ice for Summer Summer, 135, 136
Leche de Tigre, 228–31
lemongrass
in Herb Stock for Olive Oil, 211
Lemongrass Kaffir Stock for Summer Summer, 135, 136
straws, 136
in Thai Stock for Thai Fighter, 115
lemon oil, in Absinthe Syrup, 55

INDEX continued

lemons
    Citrus Oleo Saccharum for Bubblegum, 95
    in Gin, 28
    in Herbal Liqueur, 40
    in Lemongrass Kaffir Stock for Summer Summer, 135
    Lemon Horchata, 222–5
    Lemon Oleo Saccharum, 223
    Lemon Pepper Syrup for Lemon Horchata, 223, 225
    in Limoncello, 235
    in Sweet Vermouth, 39

licorice root extract,
    in Coffee Chicory Stock for Room for Dessert?, 183

limes
    Cardamom Lime Stock for Tzatziki, 219
    in Chicha Morada, 213
    Clarified Lime Cucumber for What Would Honeydew, 71, 73
    in Jamaican Rum, 37
    in Lemongrass Kaffir Stock for Summer Summer, 135
    Lime Peel Stock for Thai Peanut Sauce, 119
    in Mezcal, 32
    in Tequila, 30

Limoncello, 234–5

liquid smoke
    in BBQ, 93
    in Mezcal, 32

Lovely Bunch, 152–5

Lychee Champagne, 194–5
    in Death in the Afternoon, 56
    in French 75, 57
    in Grapefruit Mimosa, 48

M

mace, in Lemon Pepper Syrup for Lemon Horchata, 223

Maguey Sweet Sap
    in Instant Oatmeal, 125
    in Korean Spiced Margarita, 83
    in Return of the Mac, 91
    in Shake Your Tamarind, 77
    in Truffled Cherry, 173

Malta Goya malt soda
    in Instant Oatmeal, 125
    in Malt Soda Reduction for Pretzel, 139

malt extract, in Breakfast Stout, 209
mandarin purée, in Gochujang Syrup for Korean Spiced Margarita, 83
mango purée, in Clarified Passionfruit Mango Stock for IPA, 160
Manhattan, Black, 59

maple syrup
    in Blueberry Pancakes, 201
    in Salted Caramel Cherry, 151

Marcona Rice Milk for Lemon Horchata, 225

Margarita, 52
    with Hot Sauce Ice, 53
    Korean Spiced Margarita, 82–3

Marinated Tomatoes for Salad, 75
mastic, in Herbal Liqueur, 40
masticating juicers, 19
McIntosh Apple Slices for Return of the Mac, 90, 91
melon, See honeydew melon; watermelon
mesh strainers, about, 19
Me & You, 156–7
Mezcal, 32
    in Margarita, 52

milk
    Banana Milk Punch for Banana Chai, 178
    Condensed Milk Pudding for Limoncello, 235
    Hong Kong Milk Tea, 220–1
    Paprika Milk Punch, 87
    Sassafras Milk for $5 Shake, 216
    in Strawberry Tomato, 192

milk, evaporated, in Hong Kong Milk Tea, 221

milk, sweetened condensed
    Condensed Milk Pudding for Limoncello, 235
    in Roasted Sweet Potato, 107

Milk for Lemon Horchata, Marcona Rice, 225

Mimosa, Grapefruit, 48

mint
    in Fernet, 41
    in Green Papaya Salad, 145
    in Herbal Liqueur, 40
    in Herb Stock for Olive Oil, 211
    Mint Honeydew Ice in What Would Honeydew, 73

mint tea
    in Cucumber Mint Stock for Tzatziki, 219
    in Smoked Strawberry Old Fashioned, 117

miso, red
    in Golden Glow, 101
    Miso Stock for Me & You, 157

mixing glasses, about, 18
modern cocktails, 65–165

molasses
    in American Whiskey, 29
    in Blackstrap Rum, 33
    in Cardamom Port, 181
    in Mole, 165
    See also pomegranate molasses

Mole, 11, 164–5
Mum's The Word, 110–12
mushrooms, in Down to Earth, 85
mustard seeds, in BBQ Stock for BBQ, 93

N

Nectarine White Grape Stock for New Millennium, 104
Negroni, 62
New Millennium, 102–5

nutmeg
    in Aromatic Bitters, 35
    in Spanish Rum, 33

O

Oated Verjus for Instant Oatmeal, 125

oats
    in Breakfast Stout, 209
    Instant Oatmeal, 124–5

Old Fashioned, Smoked Strawberry, 116–17

oleo saccharum
    Citrus Oleo Saccharum for Bubblegum, 95, 97
    Lemon Oleo Saccharum, in Lemon Pepper Syrup for Lemon Horchata, 223

olive brine, in Salad, 75
Olive Oil, 210–11
Onion Garlic Purée for Leche De Tigre, 229, 230
Orange Bitters, 34
orange flower water, in What Would Honeydew, 73

Orange Liqueur, 31
    in Margarita, 52

orange oil, in Fruitcake Ice for Sparkling Plum Sour, 79

oranges
    in Amaro, 38
    in Aromatic Bitters, 35
    in Bitter Apéritif for Americano, 131
    in Bitter Liqueur, 42
    Bitter Orange Tincture for Peach Shrub, 197
    Citrus Oleo Saccharum for Bubblegum, 95
    Curry Blood Oranges for Lovely Bunch, 153, 155
    in Down to Earth, 85
    in Herbal Liqueur, 40
    Orange Bitters, 34
    Orange Liqueur, 31
    in Paprika Milk Punch, 87
    in Roasted Sweet Potato, 107
    in Room for Dessert?, 183
    in Spanish Rum, 33
    in Sweet Vermouth, 39

INDEX *continued*

P

Paloma, 49
Papaya Salad, Green, 144–5
paprika, smoked sweet
    Paprika Milk Punch, 86–7
    in Walnut Paprika Syrup for Salad, 75
parsley
    in Green Herb Vinegar for Green Herb Shrub, 203
    in Herbal Liqueur, 40
    in Mezcal, 32
    in Peach Vinegar for Peach Shrub, 197
    in Tequila, 30
passionfruit
    Clarified Passionfruit Mango Stock for IPA, 160
    in Golden Glow, 101
    in Peanut Butter & Banana Sandwich, 227
    Self-Carbonating Cinnamon Passionfruit Fizz, 147
passionfruit tea, in Bubblegum, 95, 97
peaches
    Peach Shrub, 196–7
    Peach Syrup for Snap Pea, 149
    Peach Vinegar for Peach Shrub, 197
peaches, dried
    in American Whiskey, 29
    in Bitter Apéritif for Americano, 131
peach nectar, in Peach Syrup for Snap Pea, 149
peach rooibos tea, in Peach Shrub, 197
peanut butter, in Green Papaya Salad, 145
Peanut Butter & Banana Sandwich, 226–7
peanut oil, grilled
    in Peanut Butter & Banana Sandwich, 227
    in Peanut Stock for Thai Peanut Sauce, 119
peanuts
    in Mezcal, 32
    in Mole, 165
    in Tequila, 30
pear juice
    in Lychee Champagne, 195
    in Spiced Pear Syrup for Americano, 131
pears, dried, in 3-Spiced Vinegar for Spiced Blueberry Shrub, 189
Pechuga, 140–1
Pectinex Ultra SP-L
    in Clarified Lime Cucumber for What Would Honeydew, 71
    in Guava Purée for Sparkling White Chocolate & Guava Consommé, 109
    in Strawberry Syrup for Smoked Strawberry Old Fashioned, 117
peelers, about, 19
peppercorns, black
    in Aromatic Bitters, 35
    Black Pepper Stock, 101
    in Herbal Liqueur, 40
    in Mezcal, 32
    in Mole, 165
    in Return of the Mac, 91
    in Tequila, 30
peppercorns, green
    in Green Herb Vinegar for Green Herb Shrub, 203
    in Herbal Liqueur, 40
peppercorns, pink, in Bitter Liqueur, 42
peppercorns, white
    in Lemon Pepper Syrup for Lemon Horchata, 223
    in Mezcal, 32
pepper flakes, red, in Coriander Stock for Pechuga, 141
peppermint extract, in Mint Honeydew Ice, 73
peppers, See bell peppers; chiles
Pepper Syrup, Lemon, for Lemon Horchata, 223
Perlini cocktail shakers, about, 18
pineapple
    in Buddha's Hand Jam for Limoncello, 235
    in Chicha Morada, 213
    in Green Papaya Salad, 145
    in Jamaican Rum, 37
    in Jungle Bird, 51
    in Mezcal, 32
    in Pechuga, 141
    in Shake Your Tamarind, 77
    in Tequila, 30
    in Thai Fighter, 115
plums
    Plum Verjus for Sparkling Plum Sour, 80, 81
    Sparkling Plum Sour, 78–81
pomegranate juice
    in Americano, 131
    Blackberry Pomegranate Syrup for Bramblin' Man, 143
    in Cereal Killer, 69
    in Return of the Mac, 91
pomegranate molasses
    in Blackberry Pomegranate Syrup for Bramblin' Man, 143
    in Roasted Sweet Potato, 107
pomegranate tea, in Roasted Sweet Potato, 107
Port, Cardamom, 181
Porthole (vessel), 89, 91
Pretzel, 13, 138–9
Prickly Pear Base for Leche de Tigre, 230
prune juice
    in Fruitcake Ice for Sparkling Plum Sour, 79
    in Mole, 165
prunes, in Fruitcake Ice for Sparkling Plum Sour, 79
pu-erh tea, in Salted Caramel Cherry, 151

R

raisins
    in Breakfast Stout, 209
    Juniper Raisin, 98–99
    in Mole, 165
    in Sun Dried, 187
    in Sweet Vermouth, 39
Return of the Mac, 88–91
Rhubarb, Thyme, Juniper, 162–3
rice
    Black Rice Stock for Self-Carbonating Cinnamon Passionfruit Fizz, 147
    Marcona Rice Milk for Lemon Horchata, 225
    Rice Milk for Peanut Butter & Banana Sandwich, 227
    Toasted Rice Stock for Blueberry Pancakes, 200, 201
Roasted Banana for Banana Chai, 177, 178
Roasted Banana Peel for Lovely Bunch, 155
Roasted Sweet Potato, 107
rooibos tea, in Peach Shrub, 197
Room for Dessert?, 182–3
root beer, in Bramblin' Man, 143
Rose Champagne, 185
rose hips
    in Grapefruit Jicama Champagne, 171
    in New Millennium, 104
    in Rose Tea Blend for Hong Kong Milk Tea, 221
Rose Noir tea, in Hong Kong Milk Tea, 221
Rose Stock for Rose Champagne, 185
rose water, in New Millennium, 104
rum, See Jamaican Rum; Spanish Rum

S

saffron
    in Fernet, 41
    in Herbal Liqueur, 40
    in Sweet Corn, 133
    Tonka Saffron Ice Cream for $5 Shake, 215
Salad, 11, 74–5
salt
    Salted Caramel Cherry, 150–1
    Salt Solution for Instant Oatmeal, 125
    Salt Solution for Rhubarb, Thyme, Juniper, 163
    Smoked Salt Solution for What Would Honeydew, 71, 73

INDEX *continued*

sandalwood, in Bitter Apéritif for Americano, 131
sarsaparilla root
    in Aromatic Bitters, 35
    in Sassafras Milk for $5 Shake, 216, 217
sassafras root
    in Aromatic Bitters, 35
    Sassafras Milk for $5 Shake, 216, 217
scale, digital, 18
Seedlip Garden 108
    in Celery Serrano, 122
    in Shake Your Tamarind, 77
    in Snap Pea, 149
    in Summer Summer, 136
    in Thai Peanut Sauce, 119
Seedlip Spice 94
    in Americano, 131
    in Cereal Killer, 69
    in Instant Oatmeal, 125
    in Lovely Bunch, 155
    in Return of the Mac, 91
    in Smoked Strawberry Old Fashioned, 117
Self-Carbonating Cinnamon Passionfruit Fizz, 146–7
sencha tea, in Strawberry Tomato, 191
separation, 21
Serrano Ice for Celery Serrano, 122
serving size, 15, 20
sesame seeds
    in Mole, 165
    in Thai Stock for Thai Fighter, 115
Shake, $5, 214–17
shakers, about, 18
Shake Your Tamarind, 76–7
shaking, dry, 21
Shrub, Grapefruit Turmeric, 174–5
Shrub, Green Herb, 202–3
Shrub, Peach, 196–7
Shrub, Spiced Blueberry, 188–9
Simple Syrup, 22
Smoked Ice Wine Tea
    for Pechuga, 141
    for Spiced Blueberry Shrub, 189
Smoked Salt Solution for What Would Honeydew, 71, 73
Smoked Strawberry Old Fashioned, 116–17
Smoke Ice for New Millennium, 103, 105
Snap Pea, 148–9
Snap Pea Syrup for Snap Pea, 149
Soft Cider, 232–3
Spanish Rum, 33
    in Daiquiri, 50
    in Jungle Bird, 51
Sparkling Plum Sour, 78–81
Sparkling White Chocolate & Guava Consommé, 108–9
Spiced Barley Stock for Cereal Killer, 69
Spiced Blueberry Shrub, 188–9
Spiced Pear Syrup for Americano, 131
Spice Mix for Paprika Milk Punch, 87
Squash Stock, Butternut, for Pretzel, 139
Stabilizer Powder for Olive Oil, 211
star anise
    in Aromatic Bitters, 35
    in Bitter Liqueur, 42
    in Falernum for Sparkling Plum Sour, 80
    in Fruitcake Ice for Sparkling Plum Sour, 79
    in Gin, 28
    in Herbal Liqueur, 40
    in Orange Bitters, 34
    Star Anise Stock for Mum's The Word, 111, 112
    in Sun Dried, 187
    in 3-Spiced Vinegar for Spiced Blueberry Shrub, 189

star anise oil, in Absinthe Syrup, 55
storage, 20
Stout, Breakfast, 208–9
straining and strainers, about, 19, 21
strawberries
    Charred Strawberries for BBQ, 93
    Strawberry Syrup for Smoked Strawberry Old Fashioned, 117
    Strawberry Tomato, 190–3
substitutions, about, 20
sumac, in Fruitcake Ice for Sparkling Plum Sour, 79
Summer Summer, 134–7
Sun Dried, 186–7
Sweet Corn, 132–3
Sweet Potato, Roasted, 106–7
Sweet Vermouth, 39
    in Bijou, 61
    in Negroni, 62
syrups
    about, 21
    basic, 22
    See also agave syrup; cane syrup; maple syrup
Szechuan peppercorns
    in Herbal Liqueur, 40
    in Mezcal, 32
    in Sun Dried, 187
    in 3-Spiced Vinegar for Spiced Blueberry Shrub, 189

T

tamari
    in Soft Cider, 233
    in Umami Bomb, 205
tamarind
    Tamarind Coriander Stock for Shake Your Tamarind, 77
    Tamarind Stock for Salted Caramel Cherry, 151
tarragon
    in Bitter Amaro, 36
    in Grapefruit Vinegar for Grapefruit Turmeric Shrub, 175
    in Green Herb Vinegar for Green Herb Shrub, 203
    in Herbal Liqueur, 40
    in Herb Stock for Olive Oil, 211
    in Sweet Vermouth, 39
tea
    in Banana Chai, 177, 178
    in Bitter Apéritif for Americano, 131
    in Bubblegum, 97
    Hong Kong Milk Tea, 220–1
    in Leche de Tigre, 229
    in Lovely Bunch, 155
    in Mum's The Word, 111, 112
    in Peach Shrub, 197
    in Pechuga, 141
    in Return of the Mac, 91
    in Roasted Sweet Potato, 107
    in Rose Champagne, 185
    in Salted Caramel Cherry, 151
    in Smoked Strawberry Old Fashioned, 117
    in Snap Pea, 149
    in Spiced Blueberry Shrub, 189
    in Strawberry Tomato, 191
    in Tzatziki, 219
Tequila, 30
    in Paloma, 49
Thai Fighter, 114–15
Thai Peanut Sauce, 118–19
Thai Stock for Thai Fighter, 115
3-Spiced Vinegar for Spiced Blueberry Shrub, 189
throwing, 21

INDEX *continued*

thyme
    in Green Herb Vinegar for Green Herb Shrub, 203
    in Herbal Liqueur, 40
    in Herb Stock for Olive Oil, 211
    in Return of the Mac, 91
    Rhubarb, Thyme, Juniper, 162–3
    Thyme Simple Syrup for Rhubarb, Thyme, Juniper, 163
Toasted Coconut for Chicha Morada, 213
Toasted Oats for Instant Oatmeal, 125
Toasted Rice Stock for Blueberry Pancakes, 200, 201
tomatoes
    in Golden Glow, 101
    Marinated Tomatoes for Salad, 75
    Strawberry Tomato, 190–3
tomatoes, green, in Salad, 75
tomatoes, sun-dried, in Chile Cardamom Stock for Cardamom Port, 181
tomatoes, yellow, in Golden Glow, 101
Tonic, Watermelon Ginger, 129
Tonka Saffron Ice Cream for $5 Shake, 215, 217
Triple Sec, See Orange Liqueur
Truffled Cherry, 172–3
Truffle Oil Stock for Truffled Cherry, 173
turmeric
    Grapefruit Turmeric Shrub, 174–5
    in Grapefruit Vinegar for Grapefruit Turmeric Shrub, 175
    Turmeric Vinegar for Watermelon Ginger Tonic, 127, 128
Tzatziki, 218–19

U
Umami Bomb, 10, 204–5

V
vadouvan, in Curry Blood Oranges for Lovely Bunch, 153
vanilla beans
    in American Whiskey, 29
    in Aromatic Bitters, 35
    in Banana Milk Punch for Banana Chai, 178
    in Falernum for Sparkling Plum Sour, 80
    in Fruitcake Ice for Sparkling Plum Sour, 79
    in Malt Soda Reduction for Pretzel, 139
    in Orange Liqueur, 31
    in Spanish Rum, 33
    in Sparkling White Chocolate & Guava Consommé, 109
    splitting and scraping, 21
    in Strawberry Tomato, 192
    in Sweet Corn, 133
    in Sweet Vermouth, 39
    in Tequila, 30
Verjus, Oated, for Instant Oatmeal, 125
Verjus, Plum, for Sparkling Plum Sour, 80, 81
verjus blanc
    in Bubblegum, 97
    in Grapefruit Jicama Champagne, 171
    in Green Papaya Salad, 145
    in Lovely Bunch, 155
    in Lychee Champagne, 195
    in Mint Honeydew Ice, 73
    in New Millennium, 104
    in Olive Oil, 211
    in Plum Verjus, 80
    in Return of the Mac, 91
    in Salad, 75
    in Summer Summer, 136
verjus rouge
    in Cardamom Port, 181
    in Fruitcake Ice for Sparkling Plum Sour, 79
    in Me & You, 157
    in Mole, 165
    in Oated Verjus for Instant Oatmeal, 125
    in Rhubarb, Thyme, Juniper, 163
    in Rose Champagne, 185
    in Sweet Vermouth, 39
    in Umami Bomb, 205
vermouth, See Sweet Vermouth
vinegar, apple cider, in 3-Spiced Vinegar for Spiced Blueberry Shrub, 189
vinegar, black, in 3-Spiced Vinegar for Spiced Blueberry Shrub, 189
vinegar, cane
    in Grapefruit Vinegar for Grapefruit Turmeric Shrub, 175
    in Green Herb Vinegar for Green Herb Shrub, 203
    in Peach Vinegar for Peach Shrub, 197
    in Turmeric Vinegar for Watermelon Ginger Tonic, 127
Vinegar, Grapefruit, 175
Vinegar, Green Herb, 203
vinegar, maple, in Salted Caramel Cherry, 151
Vinegar, Peach, 197
vinegar, rice wine, in Korean Spiced Margarita, 83
vinegar, sherry, in Marinated Tomatoes for Salad, 75
Vinegar, 3-Spiced, 189
Vinegar, Turmeric, 127, 128

W
Walnut Paprika Syrup for Salad, 75
walnuts
    in Mole, 165
    Walnut Paprika Syrup, 75
water, diluting, 15, 16
water, sparkling
    in Americano, 131
    in Snap Pea, 149
    in Watermelon Ginger Tonic, 129
watermelon
    Lavender Watermelon Ice for Summer Summer, 135, 136
    in Mum's The Word, 112
    in Smoke Ice (var.), 103
    Watermelon Ginger Tonic, 10, 126–9
    Watermelon Syrup for Watermelon Ginger Tonic, 127, 128
What Would Honeydew, 16, 70–3
Whipped Cream for $5 Shake, 217
whiskey, See American Whiskey
Whiskey Sour, 58
White Chocolate & Guava Consommé, Sparkling, 108–9
White Chocolate Syrup for Room for Dessert?, 183
wine
    about, 169
    recipes, 169–205

X
xanthan gum
    in Peanut Butter & Banana Sandwich, 227
    in Stabilizer Powder for Olive Oil, 211

Y
Yeasted Herb Stock for Soft Cider, 233
Yeast Stock for Rose Champagne, 185
Yogurt, Cardamom, for Tzatziki, 219
yuzu juice
    in Me & You, 157
    in Thai Peanut Sauce, 119
yuzu kosho, in Korean Spiced Margarita, 83
yuzu marmalade, in Gochujang Syrup for Korean Spiced Margarita, 83

THANK YOU!

Creating this volume has inherently been a labor of love; we are filled with gratitude to those who have helped us realize our vision for it.

Nick Kokonas and **Grant Achatz** have forged – not just a restaurant group – but an artist collective in which unique, unlikely, and interesting projects such as this are not only made possible, but encouraged. It's in this environment that creatives from wildly different walks of life collaborate and exchange ideas, chasing what interests them and elevating their work to the highest levels of quality. Participating in this hive is exhilarating, challenging, and supremely-gratifying; we are grateful for the opportunity to share some of their work with the world.

This book contains recipes and techniques contributed by many members of our staff, both past and present. We owe a large debt of thanks to **Micah Melton, Ingi Sigurdsson, Alexis Tinoco, Alyssa Heidt, Jarmell Doss, Bobby Murphy,** and all of our chefs who have dedicated care and attention to The Alinea Group's ever-widening non-alcoholic beverage experiments. Designing the drinks featured in these pages has taken an enormous amount of invention and effort over many years, and these recipes represent but a glimpse into a much more expansive world which they explore daily.

It's been the cheerful organizational efforts of **Alex Hayes** that have helped keep this project on pace and on budget. We are grateful for his constant help and encouragement.

On any given day, members of the **entire Alinea Group** have helped us in our efforts while maintaining the standard of service and cuisine that makes such a book possible. It cannot be overstated that without such a passionate group of dedicated people, there would be no reason for this book. We are deeply indebted to each of them.

— ALLEN & SARAH

COLOPHON

This first edition, first printing of
Zero: A New Approach to Non-Alcoholic Drinks
was printed by Shenzhen Artron Color Printing Co. Ltd.
of Shenzhen, China.

Prepress by iocolor, LLC of Seattle, Washington.

Design and photography by Sarah & Allen Hemberger.
Small Batch Creative, LLC | www.smallbatchcreative.com
art@smallbatchcreative.com

Published by:
The Alinea Group, LLC | www.thealineagroup.com

Printed using Chroma Centric HUV inks on 140 gsm Dadong woodfree FSC paper. Typefaces used include Twentieth Century, Grad, and FF Mark.

Copyright © 2020 by The Alinea Group.

All rights reserved. No portion of this book may be reproduced in any form or by any means, except for brief excerpts for the purposes of review, without the prior written permission of the author.

ISBN-13: 978-1-7330088-1-5